THE PATHETIC FALLACY

A STUDY OF CHRISTIANITY

LIST OF VOLUMES PUBLISHED IN THIS SERIES

Each bound in clothette, 1s. net.

1. **First and Last Things.** By H. G. WELLS.
2. **Education.** By HERBERT SPENCER.
3. **The Riddle of the Universe.** By ERNST HAECKEL.
4. **Humanity's Gain from Unbelief.** By CHARLES BRADLAUGH.
5. **On Liberty.** By JOHN STUART MILL.
6. **A Short History of the World.** By H. G. WELLS.
7. **Autobiography of Charles Darwin.**
8. **The Origin of Species.** By CHARLES DARWIN. (6th Copyright edition.)
9. **Twelve Years in a Monastery.** By JOSEPH MCCABE.
10. **History of Modern Philosophy.** By A. W. BENN.
11. **Gibbon on Christianity.** Being Chapters XV and XVI of Edward Gibbon' *Decline and Fall of the Roman Empire.*
12. **The Descent of Man.** Pt. I and concluding Chapter Pt. III. By CHARLES DARWIN
13. **History of Civilization in England.** By H. T. BUCKLE. Vol. I.
14 & 15. **Anthropology.** By SIR EDWARD B. TYLOR. Two vols.
16. **Iphigenia.** Two plays by EURIPIDES. English version by C. B. BONNER, M.A
17. **Lectures and Essays.** By THOMAS HENRY HUXLEY.
18. **The Evolution of the Idea of God.** By GRANT ALLEN.
19. **An Agnostic's Apology.** By SIR LESLIE STEPHEN, K.C.B.
20. **The Churches and Modern Thought.** By VIVIAN PHELIPS.
21. **Penguin Island.** By ANATOLE FRANCE.
22. **The Pathetic Fallacy.** By LLEWELYN POWYS.
23. **Historical Trials (a Selection).** By SIR JOHN MACDONELL.
24. **A Short History of Christianity.** By JOHN M. ROBERTSON.
25. **The Martyrdom of Man.** By WINWOOD READE.
26. **Head Hunters; Black, White, and Brown.** By A. C. HADDON.
27. **The Evidence for the Supernatural.** By IVOR LL. TUCKETT.
28. **The City of Dreadful Night, and Other Poems.** By JAMES THOMSON ("B. V.").
29. **In the Beginning.** By PROF. SIR G. ELLIOT SMITH, F.R.S.
30. **Adonis; A Study in the History of Oriental Religion.** By SIR JAMES G. FRAZEI
31. **Our New Religion.** By the RT. HON. H. A. L. FISHER.
32. **On Compromise.** By JOHN VISCOUNT MORLEY, O.M., P.C.
33. **History of the Taxes on Knowledge.** By COLLET DOBSON COLLET.
34. **The Existence of God.** By JOSEPH MCCABE.
35. **The Story of the Bible.** By MACLEOD YEARSLEY, F.R.C.S.
36. **Savage Survivals.** By J. HOWARD MOORE.
37. **The Revolt of the Angels.** By ANATOLE FRANCE.
38. **The Outcast.** By WINWOOD READE.
39. **Penalties Upon Opinion.** By HYPATIA BRADLAUGH BONNER.
40. **Oath, Curse, and Blessing.** By E. CRAWLEY.
41. **Fireside Science.** By SIR E. RAY LANKESTER, F.R.S. Prepared by SURGEO REAR-ADMIRAL BEADNELL.
42. **History of Anthropology.** By A. C. HADDON.
43. **The World's Earliest Laws.** By CHILPERIC EDWARDS.
44. **Fact and Faith.** By PROF. J. B. S. HALDANE.
45. **Men of the Dawn.** By DOROTHY DAVISON.
46. **The Mind in the Making.** By JAMES HARVEY ROBINSON.
47. **The Expression of the Emotions in Man and Animals.** By CHARLES DARWI Revised and Abridged by SURG. REAR-ADML. BEADNELL.
48. **Psychology for Everyman (and Woman).** By A. E. MANDER.
49. **The Religion of the Open Mind.** By A. GOWANS WHYTE.
50. **Letters on Reasoning.** By JOHN M. ROBERTSON.
51. **The Social Record of Christianity.** By JOSEPH MCCABE.
52. **Five Stages of Greek Religion.** By PROF. GILBERT MURRAY.
53. **The Life of Jesus.** By ERNEST RENAN.
54. **Selected Works of Voltaire.** Translated by JOSEPH MCCABE.
55. **What Are We to Do with Our Lives?** By H. G. WELLS.
56. **Do What You Will.** By ALDOUS HUXLEY.
57. **Clearer Thinking: Logic for Everyman.** By A. E. MANDER.
58. **History of Ancient Philosophy.** By A. W. BENN.
59. **Your Body: How it is Built and How it Works.** By DR. D. STARK MURRAY.
60. **What is Man?** By MARK TWAIN.
61. **Man and His Universe.** By JOHN LANGDON-DAVIES.
62. **First Principles.** By HERBERT SPENCER. (Double Vol., cloth, 2s. net.)

The Thinker's Library, No. 22.

THE PATHETIC FALLACY

A STUDY OF CHRISTIANITY

BY

LLEWELYN POWYS

FOLCROFT LIBRARY EDITIONS / 1977

The Thinker's Library, No. 22.

THE PATHETIC FALLACY

A STUDY OF CHRISTIANITY

BY

LLEWELYN POWYS

LONDON:

WATTS & CO.,

5 & 6 JOHNSON'S COURT, FLEET STREET, E.C.4

First published, 1930
Included in the Thinker's Library, June, 1931
Second Impression, November, 1934
Third Impression, 1937

Printed and Published in Great Britain by C. A. Watts & Co. Limited,
5 & 6 Johnson's Court, Fleet Street, London, E.C.4

DEDICATED TO

CLARENCE DARROW

WITH AFFECTION AND APPRECIATION

The Rationalist Press Association Ltd. desire to thank Messrs. Longmans, Green & Co. Ltd. for their kind permission to include this volume in the Thinker's Library.

PREFATORY NOTE TO THIS EDITION

EVERY living religious faith has a strong personal element. Even in the Roman Catholic Church, which seeks to impose uniformity in every detail of belief, individual differences show through the rigid texture of the Creed.

In this little book Mr. Powys reveals his own reactions to the claims of Christianity. Deeply aware of the power which this religion has wielded for two thousand years, he yet finds it wanting as a guide to the human spirit. His verdict is all the more impressive since he bases his judgment on what may be called the face value of the records, and not on the latest and most destructive speculations of Biblical scholars.

Seldom do writers deal with this familiar theme in such vivid and poetic language as Mr. Powys has at command. His picturesque style, no less than his originality and sincerity, make *The Pathetic Fallacy* a stimulating and delightful book.

May, 1931.

CONTENTS

THE PATHETIC FALLACY

CHAPTER I

THE ORIGIN OF ALL RELIGIONS

In considering any religion it would seem advisable to carry always in our minds the ultimate origin of such psychic manifestations. Christianity must take its place with the rest. In its lowest gravitation it has sprung from the shuddering of the living human spirit in the face of the Infinite. Nations, however vigorous they may be, however occupied with their objective matter-of-fact world condition, sooner or later have to devise some means by which they may accommodate themselves to the unanswerable mysteries of that physical universe which forms the amphitheatre for their wilful ambitions. At the death of any man, whether it takes place in a palace or in a cockle-loft, the minds of those who attend are brought up "in short order" before an importunate problem. Every corpse is a stiff interrogator. It is so to-day, and it has been so since consciousness first separated our kind from the anthropoid apes. All moralities, all philosophies, all religions, are a direct product of death. As toadstools grow up from buried logs so do these fantasies take their nourishment from buried bones.

Some compensating explanation has to be sought for the swift passing of the generations. Not even a Pharaoh, a Cæsar, or a Tamburlaine can reconcile himself to an existence inconsequent and empty of meaning. The egoism of the species is involved. Let the lives of pismires, of pygargs, be without significance, but not those of cardinal man.

It has been well said that religion grew out of fear, fear of nature, fear of super-nature, fear of death. We are ever at pains to send up incense clouds so that we can engage in our pushing activities out of sight of the awful eye of God. As often as we see a dead body we are reminded of our lot and must needs set about chanting, ringing bells, and marching in procession. Like spiders, with express diligence we spin out webs and trust to restore our hardihood behind veils of our own slender creation.

The existence of consciousness, even in its rudest form, would seem to presuppose a belief in the supernatural. Our ancestors, as they dropped from trees on the flat palms of their feet, or emerged blinking from their caves, or sat chipping at their flints with legs outstretched, could not fail to be vividly reminded of the wonder of creation. An unexplained footfall, a chance shadow, an echo even, would stimulate uncertain imaginings. And if they remained gross under such indeterminate influences, which of them could be indifferent to the audible roaring of thunder, or to the importunacy of a corpse lying in their vicinity hour after hour, without sight, or breath, or argument? Some of us to-day are content to find the secret of life in poetry, and acknowledge thereby that wonder remains still the homage that our nature pays to the unknown. The uninterrupted majesty of the sun's diurnal progress, the monthly movements of the moon, the stars in their midnight multiplicity, compel us towards moods of religion. The veriest dolt catches something sublime in the perishable beauty of the objective world in summer-time, when butterflies, those painted, boneless insects, flit from flower head to flower head! The mystery of existence engenders a feeling of awe, and in such "spiritual" states gods grow up as common as docks in a hedge-row. Such plausible beings offer good service in hours of perplexity. Their assumed existence suggests ready solutions. Our amazement is soothed. All is made clear.

CHAPTER II

THE HEBREW ROOT OF CHRISTIANITY

THE ultimate origin of Christianity is to be found in the infinity of the haughty heavens, in the mystery of the earth, and in the recurrent cunning of corpses. Its immediate origin is to be looked for in the history of the Jews. No race has been so God-intoxicated as this extraordinary people. From the earliest times they have realized God. He has been an obsession with them. Though the Egyptians had already conceived the idea of a single supreme deity, " the one that was all "; though the Babylonians had upon occasion raised Marduk into a position of sovereign solitude, it was the Jews who, with an outburst of religious inspiration, converted the Yahweh of Sinai into a universal ruler. There had, of course, been militant tribal gods before the appearance of Yahweh; but none of these had been able to combine the prowess of war with a concern for the moral ordering of the world, with a concern for the welfare of the downtrodden, of women, and of orphans. Could any change of heart be more surprising? Did His own prophets put such magnanimity into God's head?

The Jews were a very vital people. They knew little of the arts and graces of life, of its finer accomplishments. Their contribution to human culture was on different lines. As the humped-back cattle of Africa will rush down to the salt lick of Lake Elmenteita so did these "Yahudis" thirst after eternity. They knew, none better, their own ruthless manners, and were fain to associate difficult moral restraints with their deity. Not only did Yahweh insist that they should worship him and him alone, but he also demanded of them righteousness. In so far as they deviated from honest conduct their national misfortunes could be explained. It was simple. God turned away His countenance from them because they had transgressed. After this manner they devised their arguments for explaining how a national omnipotent protector could suffer His chosen people to be so tormented. If they, like so many dutiful asses, had known their master's crib, if their scales had been justly balanced, if they had been obedient to clothe the poor and feed the fatherless, then Nebuchadnezzar's cohorts would never have been allowed to carry them away captive.

No race but the Jews, with the obstinacy of pigs and the idealism of saints, could have retained their belief during those years of desolate exile in Babylon. Such a national disaster would have soured the faith of any other people. Jerusalem had been razed, its walls thrown down, its gates burnt, the temple of Solomon reduced to a heap of ruined stones, and yet under the spell of Ezekiel, that prophet "disguised in a priest's mantle," they maintained their illusion. They did more, they began to brood over, and to assimilate into their national consciousness, certain wild words that had been spoken by their prophets, words that seemed to foretell a revival of their nation under the rule of a prince of the house of David. The pride of the Jews invented this idea.

They were captives, slaves, impotent and abject. There seemed to be no issue to their tribulations. When lo! these vain-glorious exiles dreamed wish-dreams converting present misery into future triumphs. Their sacred writings became heavy with strange oracular utterances.

One of the most urgent preoccupations of the early Christians was to illustrate clearly that the ancient Messianic prophecies pointed to the coming of Jesus. To the Jews and to the unbelieving these elaborate interpretations have always seemed far-fetched. And this lack of confidence has been accentuated by the fact that several passages of the New Testament scriptures show unmistakable evidence of having been written up to fulfil these same early predictions. It is well known that learned Rabbis versed in the ancient canons of their race have singularly failed to find credible connexion between the long-looked-for Messiah-king of the prophets, and the Galilean preacher who was put to death by Pontius Pilate. "The revolution of seventeen centuries has instructed us not to press too closely the mysterious language of prophecy and revelation." Yet that these obscure passages were from the first intimately connected with the rise of Christianity cannot be disputed; albeit for us at the present time their chief importance lies in the fact that *Jesus Himself took them to refer to Himself.* The point is that these inspired words, so full of hope and compassion, and of the certitude of a wide redemption, put into the head of Jesus His unusual idea. They were the utterance of a proud and deeply religious people, threatened, broken, ruined. Only with such winged words upon their lips could they possibly face the future. The misery of their exile had been succeeded by other national disasters. Antiochus had tortured them. The hand of Herod the Great had fitted an iron yoke about their necks. In the actual ordinary world they could look for no issue. Small wonder, therefore, that the imaginings of these ancient "sages of Israel" became lodged in their minds. Their words, permeated with strange mystical innuendoes, must be true. Sooner or later the nation's troubles would have an end. Its agony would suddenly be transformed. A golden age would replace the iron age of the Romans. The pangs of the Messiah would give way to a period of victorious peace, and a descendant of David would sit once more upon the throne of David. The world would end, the world would be redeemed, and the prolonged travail of their race would at the last be justified.

The Messianic prophecies are remarkable. If they had been confined to predictions of a worldly kingdom they would have coincided with reason. They do not. Many prophets, but especially Isaiah, harbour the strange conjecture that salvation will come through suffering and sacrifice. It was a notion closely connected with the Jews' favourite time-honoured method of justifying the rulings of their God, whose punishments were for a purpose, and, indeed, did but ensure His final mood of forgiveness. Yet even when we have finished considering these paragraphs under the light of reason, when we have examined them, looked them up and down, these uncommon jots and tittles so carefully preserved on sheepskins and papyrus rolls, our minds yet retain a modicum of mistrust, as though in actual fact they might be verily found to hold a ghostly rumour.

Undoubtedly the spiritual interpretations of the Messianic idea were developed from the cruder ambition. Yet as the two notions often appear concurrently in the same prophet it is not always easy to trace out their gradual separation. In the following quotations the longing for a worldly Davidic kingdom may be clearly recognized. "In that day will I raise up the tabernacle of David that is fallen, and close up the breaches thereof; and I will raise up his ruins, and I will build it as in the days of old" (Amos ix. 11). "Afterward shall the children of Israel return, and seek the Lord their God, and David their king; and shall fear the Lord and his goodness in the latter days" (Hosea iii. 5). "But they shall serve the Lord their God, and David their king, whom I will raise up unto them" (Jeremiah xxx. 9). "And I will set up one shepherd over them, and he shall feed them, even my servant David; he shall feed them, and he shall be their shepherd. And I the Lord will be their God, and my servant David a prince among them; I the Lord have spoken it" (Ezekiel xxxiv. 23, 24).

These prophecies are obviously the expression of the patriotic desires of a people mightily oppressed. They are in no way mystical. The reign of David marked a period of the united glory of the Hebrew race, and these sentences formulated a consorted longing that it would happen again. In post-exilic days when the hope of a political restoration under a sovereign of the traditional line appeared less and less possible, interest in these old kingly prophecies gradually transformed itself into more consecrated yearnings. The coming of a Messiah before whose power, unaided by the sword, evil would be vanquished and an epoch of universal peace would be inaugurated, became all their thought. Under oppression the idea flourished, until in the days of Herod the Great a belief in this sublime Messiah became the common property of the nation. It was as much in the minds of the punctilious Pharisees as they passed through the temple courts as in the minds of the mule-drivers as they followed their burdened animals along the stony roads. The sullen rocks of the land, the sacred fig trees with their sprawling supplicating branches, the tender coloured flowers which for but a single day illumined the landscape, all spoke of it. The idea was afloat in the very dust of Palestine. Those who could read looked into the Scriptures and there they found it ever recurring, like the sound of a mighty sea, deep and strong and charged with assurances of an infinite release. "Rejoice greatly, O daughter of Zion; shout, O daughter of Jerusalem: behold, thy King cometh unto thee: he is just, and having salvation; lowly, and riding upon an ass, and upon a colt the foal of an ass" (Zechariah ix. 9). "Comfort ye, comfort ye my people, saith your God. . . . The voice of him that crieth in the wilderness, Prepare ye the way of the Lord, make straight in the desert a highway for our God. . . . And the glory of the Lord shall be revealed, and all flesh shall see it together: for the mouth of the Lord hath spoken it" (Isaiah xl. 1–5). "But thou, Bethlehem Ephratah, though thou be little among the thousands of Judah, yet out of thee shall he come forth unto me that is to be ruler in Israel; whose goings forth have been from of old, from everlasting" (Micah v. 2).

CHAPTER III

JESUS OF NAZARETH

JESUS was born when Augustus was emperor and was executed in the reign of his successor, Tiberius, that man. of "mud mixed from blood." Rome, partly by the accident of opportunity, partly by the ability of her people, had come to dominate all the nations of the known world. A materialistic view of life was natural to the Romans. Their values were cash values. This statement may be supported by the fact that their greatest contribution to Western civilization is found in their highly-developed sense of justice. They had a genius for dealing efficiently with everyday affairs. They had the highest sense of organization. Their gift for government can find an analogy in their great roads which stretched themselves forward to the ends of the earth, regardless of obstacles. Yet on any other plane but that of the work-a-day world they were artless vulgarians. No sooner, therefore, had they won the kingdoms by the strength of the sword than they themselves were spiritually vanquished by the prevailing cultures of those kingdoms. Every philosophy, every religion, found its way to Rome. Like rooks in autumn gathering to a king rookery so did these phantom insubstantial creations of the human mind close in upon the victorious city. Generations passed, and presently that ghostly flock of superstitions infected the natures of these men of action with a deep and unsettling restlessness. They in their turn began to worship strange gods. The sensuality of the East sapped their vigour. Gone for ever was the harmless gaiety of the Greek Eros; it had been replaced by what was heartless and gross and commercial. There is something singularly repellent about the Roman attitude to these things. How destructive to the grace of the sex illusion are the great clumsy phallic signs to be seen to-day over the common stews in the streets of Pompeii! The Romans ordered their pleasures wholesale without restraint or discrimination. Their pleasures were rich men's pleasures; sensuality was rendered worthless by satiety. They never learned that the rarest delights that mortal can experience are not to be bought or sold. I recollect seeing in a house of Pompeii a coloured representation of a huge, heavy, half-erect, drooping, uncircumcised cod-piece weighed in a pair of scales against a heap of golden coins. No pious sermon against the abuse of primitive impulses could have been more persuasive. Looking at that mural picture it became apparent to me as never before that the true secret of life does not lie in unrestrained sexual indulgence.

Herod the Great, that Idumæan slave, represented in his jurisdiction and in his person a fine example of Roman brutality. He philandered with Hellenistic traditions, but at the same time never forgot that his sovereignty ultimately depended upon the Roman rod. Yet any estimate of his career would be one-sided if his peculiar individual genius were to be overlooked. He had in his veins strange blood. He was driven by the passions of his desert ancestry. He was froward, superstitious, cursed. Firm and frightful in his outward dealings with men, his inner being was hunted and haunted. There can be no doubt that Herod the Great ploughed the soil for the spring corn of Christianity. No restharrow impeded that terrible coulter until all was ready. It was his ferocious administration that drove the spirit of the Hebrews back upon itself. Material values, a material conception of life, ruthless and without restraint, were predominant, and it was inevitable that a reaction would set in. The body had conquered, but the oppressed soul was not dead. The times were ripe for a new subversive revolution. There was a power abroad more insidious than money, mightier than the sword; a secret, lively power that, although it had been crushed and crushed again, still lived on with the tenacity of a worm cut in several parts.

The Jews saw majestic Pagan buildings rise up in all directions upon the sacred soil of the land God "sware unto them"; they saw their new temple, "Herod's building," as they grudgingly called it, dominating their Holy City. They were massacred, tortured, pestered with tax-gatherers; yet all this suffering had the effect of driving them back for nourishment upon their own secrets. They bowed their heads and brooded upon their lore. They remembered God, their own God, more powerful and more merciful than any Pagan deity, they remembered the mad murmurings of their own possessed prophets. All the banked-up traditions of their theocratic reliance surged through their obstinate beings. The world was "out of joint." Deliverance must be at hand. A miracle would happen, must happen. If they waited long enough upon the Lord, if they repented and exercised with still greater fervour their moral preconceptions, then the Messiah would come and with him salvation. Their desperate necessity caused them to elaborate their irrational hopes. A whole literature sprang up having to do with doctrines of last things. If they could hold still to the secret paths of their ancient teachings, then surely the very heavens would crack! To all appearance the province of Jewry was developing as other tracts of land under the suzerainty of Rome; in reality the dwellers upon its surface were quick with unsubjugated premonitions. Throughout the length and breadth of the country, from Hebron to Jacob's Well, from Nazareth to the Dead Sea, the minds of this peculiar people were preoccupied with impossible hopes.

Jesus was born some time during the last years of the reign of Herod the Great; was born, perhaps, in the house of a common carpenter high up in the hills of Galilee; was born, perhaps, at the very time when the sinister king was dying at Jericho like a leopard grown foul, panting at the back of its cave.

The two great influences that went to form the character of Jesus were the sacred Scriptures and the simple sights of the country. It is abundantly evident that He applied Himself to the study of the Psalms and of the Law and of the Prophets with the greatest diligence. He had a quick intellectual apprehension, but what was more important still was His spiritual responsiveness which made it possible for Him, with the unstriving sureness of genius, to understand the religious divination that lay beneath the emotion of the ancient words. Driven back upon

Himself by outward circumstances He assimilated the inner wisdom of the scrolls He read. His soul took shelter in the writings of His ancestors, yet they did not cloy His mind. He did not acquire knowledge of them as did so many erudite Pharisees for the sake of that knowledge. He drank from those words of exalted assurance as a thirsty man drinks from water springing freshly from a fountain. All this wealth of blessed utterance He made His own, and applied it without artifice to the everyday world about Him. In doing this He was helped and influenced by the simple environment of His upbringing. Close contact with natural scenes is a mighty protection against the conceit of pedantry. In later times the strength and beauty of His teaching were dependent to a very large extent upon these early impressions. It was because He Himself had seen and heard and touched the perishable objects of the natural world that His lessons were so convincing, as convincing as only the pure poetry of the senses can be. Coming out of His habitation as the sun went down He would mark how the circuit of the clouds glowed with red over Mount Carmel; crossing a slanting place of dry mud He would observe the anxious concern that His neighbour's hen would show gathering her chickens to her and outspreading her wings over the littered ground. In the mornings He would follow that lovely upland track that runs above Nazareth, and as He picked His way over the ruts, would observe how the tares were entangled with the tall, thin barley of those cultivated acres; He would watch the small wild birds with eyes of consideration for their individual existences, the sheep and goats He would observe, and the tethered wayside asses. He noted the water bursting out of the village spring, so cool, so transparent, and so *living*. He was acquainted with the taste, with the smell of the fruit of the vine. He meditated upon the personalities of the people about Him until He had learned to discount the outward presentation, and with a single glance, or a single word, could reveal the inner hidden being. His perceptions were unfailing, His insights certain. Whether it was Herod or an harlot who stood before Him, nothing was hid. He comprehended the grace of spirit that lay behind the blandishments of the girl just as readily as He understood the pathos of the Tetrarch's portentous presence. There are many dreams that can only exist in temples, churches, and libraries; His dreams live on in squares and thoroughfares and market-places. They have to do with life, they are made out of life, and considering the general bent of His teaching this thing is a great anomaly.

It was His meeting with John the Baptist that first put into the mind of Jesus the dangerous and audacious belief that it was He Himself, and no other, who was the long-expected Messiah. We can never tell what exactly happened at that river bank, what passed between those two remarkable Semitics as they stood knee to knee in the sacred stream. Did they know what they were doing? Did the older man, the rude, rough prophet, caught up in a whirlwind, look for one hesitating second with significant suspended consciousness into the eyes of the other? There had already been Jews who had taken upon themselves to be the worldly champions of their race, and the fable of the Temptation would seem to suggest that for a short period something of a like purpose came into Christ's mind also, soon, however, to be discarded for this other plan of His own devising. He had studied the Scriptures in such a way that He not only understood, but actually *felt* their meaning. He had pondered over those great chapters of Isaiah which symbolized the sufferings of the Jews in the form of a servant who through willing endurance wins for the nation a state of blessed redemption. In some obscure way this idea may also have been associated in His mind with the notion of sacrifice which the long centuries of temple worship at Jerusalem had made so familiar. At the beginning of His mission He does not seem to have been very clear as to what He intended, yet it is evident that in the more illuminated moments of His life, when He was alone, or when He prayed, He knew of a surety that He was the "Blessed one" who by preaching repentance and a return to righteousness would hasten the coming of "the last days," and who, so He eventually came to believe, would be chosen when the heavens opened to sit on the right hand of "Power." Whatever explanations may be given for what happened it cannot be disputed that the mind of Jesus, with all its mysticism, was singularly childlike. Indeed, the tragedy of the Crucifixion was the direct outcome of a reasoning as irrational as it was magnanimous.

The fifty-third chapter of the Book of Isaiah would seem to have especially inspired Him. These oracular verses have fascinated the commentators of successive generations. Their very obscurity is provocative of interest. In these lofty words we find consciously developed the idea of vicarious sacrifice, the idea of the redemption of the guilty through the anguish of the innocent. They had been begotten of the old theory that the misfortunes of the Jews as a nation had been imposed upon them for a moral purpose. By such a winnowing could the golden grain alone be separated. Brought to birth out of a reality hard to be explained, this idea of deputed punishment presently took the form of a despised and rejected person who in some mystical way, under no compulsion except a secret, silent, heroical impulse, voluntarily offered up Himself as a lamb upon an altar. Though the notion in its inception was essentially barbarous, yet an attempt to make practical use of it postulated a spiritual altruism that in the history of the world can never be regarded as anything but startling. The seed of the idea accorded with the alarmed superstitious impulses of the Neanderthal man "in his dark cloud making his moan," but its practical application drew near to the sublime.

It is extraordinary to think that these Christmas words, so familiar to us, must have been considered and reconsidered by Jesus—words caught out of the air and borne down the ages from mouth to mouth.

"Who hath believed our report? and to whom is the arm of the Lord revealed? For he shall grow up before him as a tender plant, and as a root out of a dry ground: he hath no form nor comeliness; and when we shall see him, there is no beauty that we should desire him. He is despised and rejected of men; a man of sorrows, and acquainted with grief: and we hid as it were our faces from him; he was despised, and we esteemed him not. Surely he hath borne our griefs, and carried our sorrows: yet we did esteem him stricken, smitten of God, and afflicted. But he was wounded for our transgressions, he was bruised for our iniquities: the chastisement of our peace was upon him; and with his stripes we are healed. All we like sheep have gone astray; we have turned every one to his own way; and the Lord hath laid on him the iniquity of us all. He was oppressed, and he was afflicted, yet he opened not his mouth: he is brought as a lamb to the slaughter, and as a sheep before her shearers is dumb, so he openeth not his mouth. He was taken from prison and from judgment: and who shall declare his generation? for he was cut off out of the land of the living: for the transgression of my people was he stricken. And he made his grave with the wicked, and with the rich in his death; because he had done no violence, neither was any deceit in his mouth. Yet it pleased the Lord to bruise him; he hath put him to grief: when thou shalt make his soul an offering for sin, he shall see his seed, he shall prolong his days, and the pleasure of the Lord shall prosper in his hand. He shall see of the travail of his soul, and shall be satisfied: by his knowledge shall my righteous servant justify many; for he shall bear their iniquities. Therefore will I divide him a portion with the great, and he shall divide the spoil with the strong; because he hath poured out his soul unto death: and he was numbered with the transgressors; and he bare the sin of many, and made intercession for the transgressors."

We are justified in conjecturing that Jesus in some secret understanding of His own, identified Himself with the heroic subject of this chapter, and this was especially the case probably when the initial success of His mission had been succeeded by the period of humiliation. He was the traditional Messiah, the consciousness of this was His life illusion. Such a conception, probably ill defined even in His own mind, formed the fortifying background to His life. What-even might occur this belief could not be threatened. It was in its nature to give sustenance to His spirit in the face of the most appalling disaster. Not by the might of the spear would the old dragon be conquered, but by the impossible power of love.

Jesus was no great philosopher. He had no wide vision of life. He interpreted the human situation as viewed from within the confines of Palestine. It would be difficult to systematize His teaching, so full of contradictions is it. Its strength lay in His personality, a personality possessed with a disarming innocence, but at the same time alive with an unaccountable passion. Ordinary values, the values of this world, never influenced Him. His " innocence " set Him apart in some curious way. There was that in Him that could not be contaminated. All those material anxieties that pester our minds like twilight gnats did not exist for Him. Till the hour of His death He was immune from all those ephemeral preoccupations that perplex and beset us. He only treated with matters which had the truth in them, yet no homely incident occurred but He saw in it " eternity in an hour." Those that came in contact with Him could never rid themselves of the love that He roused in their hearts. The simplicity of His genius held them enthralled. No homage could make this man vain who throughout His life remained vulnerable to each new turn of events, and yet who never, not for a single moment, lost the integrity of His inner being; no homage can be great enough with which to honour Him. It was the intense personal adoration provoked by His unique individuality that rendered the rise of Christianity possible.

When He was dead and could no more look over His shoulder at the sun, when His life had been taken from Him, and the particular tone of His voice could never again be heard, the power of His mysterious person still remained unabated. All that was tender, all that was sensitive and nervous, all that was opposed to the harsh claims of triumphant matter, rallied to the rumour of this unlikely prophet. From the first the spiritual assurances that He Himself had felt were communicated to others. Was this the hint, the word, that the hungry generations had waited for? Immediately upon its presentation a restlessness was observed and there appeared in many places and in many manners that strange myth, simple, subtle, dangerous, and sublime.

Yet though so large a portion of the human race has believed in Jesus, few have been able to put His preaching into practice. There is indeed something essentially impractical about it. Taken literally it is not applicable to the rude workings of the world. Perhaps Jesus Himself realized that life is wavering and blind, and that truth is to be found in a comprehension of opposites. Certainly, in the account we have of His sayings we can be sure of no consistent or accurate doctrine. We receive the impression of a certain temper of mind, that is all; a temper of mind radical and yet at the same time deeply spiritual.

> What was the sound of Jesus's breath?
> He laid His hand on Moses' law;
> The ancient Heavens, in silent awe,
> Writ with curses from pole to pole,
> All away began to roll.

If we try with complete honesty to make stand out the more important disclosures of His attitude we shall find that He vigorously admonishes us to be unreconciled to the world, deliberately to court misfortune and suffering, in so far as the true values as He sees them are endangered by such worldly considerations as desire, ambition, and success. No teacher has ever laid down a narrower way for his disciples, and none from the first has been less obeyed. Yet even this general drift of His teaching can be contradicted, and it may well be that the strength of His gospel lies in its latent power of infinite interpretation. The intellect can get no coherent sense out of these pages, and yet in these accidental sayings it is possible for even the heart of an atheist to respond as though he had been permitted to hear, against all expectation, divine words. The soul, the soul of man, was all His care. His hatred of hypocrisy was an obsession with Him. He had a prejudice against anything that was strict and formal and subservient to the copybook laws of society. A mean soul He could smell from afar off like a bad fish. He definitely preferred a fornicator, an adulterer, a good bad man to the sanctimonious self-righteous. Have no doubt of it, He was not unconversant with the existence of "heathen goodness," that goodness which looks for no rewards and fears no punishments, but which blesses the fields of the earth like sunshine. "The publicans and the harlots go into the kingdom of heaven before you." How it has come about that in these times we associate the name of Jesus with unpleasant people of "stupid being" I know not. They have taken Him by perfidy; and by force they have locked Him up in their churches.

From the beginning Christianity has been perverted. Theologians and priests and conventional householders have given many an ill term to its doctrines. Down the ages it has been their constant purpose to appropriate these free words to their own usage. The values of such people are transitory values. They are at pains to preserve society as it is. The deeper, more dangerous, intimations that have to do with eternity they consistently ignore. Like carrion birds they grow fat out of the commodities of death. The strength of the priest lies in man's fear of mortality. He is not concerned with any daring or dangerous state of heightened consciousness. He endeavours to enclose men's minds within the compass of his own vision. Nothing could be further from the purpose of Jesus. The thing is apparent. It has been apparent to the saints. Jesus hated dead estimates. All those depressing surface standards of the commonplace, unillumined world He could not abide. What such "home-guards" extolled He hated. The only kinds of people He execrated were the strict moralists, the petty-minded priests of His day, the sly, conventional oppressors. He turned from them. He showed openly that He preferred the company of whores to theirs. "The sins which occupied the attention of Jesus were hypocrisy, worldliness, intolerance, and selfishness: the sins which occupy the principal attention of the church, as everybody knows from experience, are impurity, murder, the excessive drinking of alcohol, swearing, and the neglect of the church services and ordinances." Ridding our minds of the traditional priestly teachings, it is possible to catch the true tenor of Christ's mood. A hundred chance utterances confirm our opinion. What does He say to the woman caught in adultery? "Neither do I condemn thee." What does He say in defence of the harlot? She is forgiven. "For she loved much." Even in the prayer that He made up, He bases our plea for forgiveness, not on any atonement that *He* was about to make, not "for Jesus Christ's sake," still less because we have taken advantage of the mystery of the church sacraments, but simply on the plea of natural human goodness. "Forgive us our trespasses, *as we forgive them that trespass against us*." What has He to say to the spiritual authorities of His time, to the men who everybody acknowledged lived strict, punctilious lives after the exact letter of the law? He called them deceitful depositories of dead men's bones, adders, and I know not what else. His attention was ever directed toward the soul of the individual and its place in the eternal plan, and He was never weary of showing that to live according to the law was not enough. It is true that He said many ignorant and foolish things. No one who contemplates our earthly existence with an emancipated mind can possibly believe that men and women, still less the sparrows in the spouting, live under the benevolent care of a human-minded God. We touch just here what good churchmen call one of the mysteries. They use the word advisedly. The fact is that the mind of Jesus was full of misconceptions. Life is not ordered by a loving father. A sucking child can see that it is not. We would all like it to be so, but that is another matter. Actually, what do we see?—dim uncertain shadows moving across apparently solid margins of beauty and terror, with below and below again, a cold and dispassionate causation transforming and retransforming all matter. A kind of underground law of gravitation is everywhere at work and no white magic has at any time altered its direction. It is absurd to believe that it has. The more we study mind and matter scientifically the more we see that all things follow a natural sequence, a sequence as liable to work for our disadvantage as for our advantage. It flows like the water of a river, it falls like rain, it is as impartial as the sea. It is as innocent of malice as it is of compassion. It is deaf to our prayers. The tender love in the heart of Jesus caused Him to believe that this was not the case. He boldly challenged the empire of matter. He insisted that eventually victory would lie with the spirit. It is stated that the question still remains open. In order to justify His confidence even Jesus found it necessary to appeal to a future existence. There can be no doubt that He constantly made use of His belief in a future life to strengthen His teaching. This belief also remains to-day a matter for controversy. The corn lands of Christianity from the first were sowed with seeds from a mixed bag, seeds of truth and seeds of falsehood.

Yet, say what we will, Jesus was no common messenger; He whispered a secret that cannot be forgot. Words like forgiveness, compassion, innocence, will always be associated with His name. With all His hasty speaking against the lake-side villages, and against the sanctimonious, He represented in a peculiar way the emotion of pity. He put into God's heart what He found in His own. Christianity is based on several illusions: the illusion of a beneficent God, the illusion that each individual soul lives after death, the illusion that Jesus Himself rose from the dead, the illusion that the world is shortly to come to an end. But yet truth remains in it.

No man has been less blinkered than Jesus, less spiritually blindfold. His reactions were always undirected—swift, sure, and unexpected. He saw life with imaginative sympathy as a poet sees it. He revealed a mystery which has never grown stale or out of date, and it is upon this spiritual mystery deriving direct from Jesus rather than from St. Paul that Christianity in all its manifold forms is ultimately founded. It grew out of truth, but it has prospered upon lies. In any rational consideration of a religion it is not only the hidden immortal seed of the faith that should command our attention, but also the dogmatic, objective claims that have sprung from that creed. Here we come upon certain legends that explain the phenomenon of what we see to-day. St. Paul was not slow to appreciate the essential value of these, and especially emphasized that absolute credence should be given to the report that Jesus had risen from the dead. This seemed to be to him the pivotal fact. "If Jesus did not rise from the dead, then is your faith in vain." Against all reason a portion of the human race has clung to this fancy. The evidence supporting it is childish, yet the continual existence of the error gives perennial proof of the eagerness with which mankind in its predicament is disposed to embrace any hope. We are like sheep who find themselves in a butcher's paddock. If one of our number has ever got through the fence there is at least a chance that others will be able to do the same near the elder tree where the brambles grow the thinnest. Certainly, if it could be absolutely proven beyond any possible doubt that the story of the resurrection was true, then all the stored industrious knowledge of humanity would weigh lightly indeed. We would have a sure demonstration that anything was possible. We would enjoy a large sense of freedom. We would know that at any time the crass circumstance of things could be reversed. We would be justified in relying upon arbitrary interventions. At any hour, in any year, our situation might be relieved by a fresh interference, a fresh illumination. A swallow might carry a message to us brushing the wind of its whisperings against our cheeks as it swept by in the open fields. Prayer might be potent to save us. The unendurable sequence of cause and effect might be considered to exist on sufferance only; to be firmly planted only as long as the miraculous did not cut through the thread of sequence. There is not evidence enough to justify such a supposition. There never has been. Too prone are we to invent such subterfuges.

The story of the crucifixion as we have it in the Gospels is written with such naïve realism that it is difficult to doubt the veracity of its main outlines. The account we have of it is certainly taken from actual recollections of that dolorous afternoon. Seldom is it possible to suspect the hand of any religious manipulator. "My God, My God, why hast Thou forsaken Me?" The deep impression that this last desperate cry made upon those who stood about the cross is proved by its preservation. One would scarcely have supposed that these were words to found a religion upon. Yet how convincingly they testify to the authenticity of the secret convictions sustaining the suffering man up to the very last moment of His life.

CHAPTER IV

THE LEGEND OF THE RESURRECTION

When I was in Palestine I overheard somebody say that there had recently been found a head that was thought to be the head of Jesus. The speaker referred, of course, to a piece of sculpture, but I for a moment really imagined that the actual skull of Christ had been casually turned up by an Arab spade after resting for two thousand years in the dry Syrian soil. My foolish mistake was soon corrected. There can, however, be little doubt that if the matter-of-fact utter truth were known the head of Jesus did moulder to dust somewhere in the vicinity of Jerusalem, that city of abused Prophets, and might indeed have been handled still intact by Titus, had that "beloved one of the human race" been directed to its obscure resting-place on the morning after the fall of Jerusalem in the year 70 A.D.

With the knowledge that we have won in recent years we are safe in asserting that no man has ever risen out of the grave. The smell of a corpse alone should be sufficient to instruct us in a better logic. How then did the story of the resurrection get spread abroad? It must be remembered that the accounts we have of it were written down long after the event was imagined to have taken place. It is useless in this book to spend time in investigating the evidence for and against it. People either believe in the resurrection of Jesus or they do not, they either know it to be true or they know it not to be true. For a lover of wisdom to accept such an occurrence the most infallible proofs would have to be accessible. They are not. All that is offered us has its origin in the dimness of an extreme antiquity. A thousand miraculous happenings have been honoured by the testimony of the ancients, which in later times under a more exacting and sceptical scrutiny can no longer be believed. Inherent in man's nature is his disposition to be gulled. What actually took place we shall never know. It is impossible to hold the theory that the rumour was the result of a deliberate invention. This religion could not have grown up out of a conscious deception. St. Peter and his companions were undoubtedly honest. Probably the women did actually find the stone rolled away. Perhaps hallucinations followed, evoked by their love. In the passage of the years these visions would tend to take firmer shape; and without perfidy the superstitious hearsay, so full of conflicting narrations, would gradually crystallize into a report coherent and credible enough to satisfy the demands of simple and unenquiring minds.

The story of Easter is a deep and tender myth created and preserved by the passionate longings of men. It is the direct product of those pitiful self-convincing intimations of immortality that intermittently taunt each one of us during our brief hours of consciousness, during those moments when in secret silent meditation the very heavens seem to open as we look with faltering souls at the dead bodies of those we have loved. After the crucifixion, indeed after the arrest of Jesus in His retreat on the Mount of

Olives, His disciples were scattered. The one they had come to follow, the one they had come to believe in, had been executed like any hedge rogue. The world remained unperturbed. The disobedient life of Jerusalem continued as if nothing had happened. The Jews elbowed their way up to Herod's building, the priests amid the sounds of trumpets and the religious outcries of the populace performed their accustomed offices. The walls of the city stood patiently solid in the same ordinary way between gate and gate. All was as it had been. The Mount of Olives preserved its natural contours. In the thronged narrow streets the mules and asses still slipped upon the pavements, so carefully grooved by the Romans. In the valley of Jehoshaphat the tomb of Absalom still presented its pointed fool's cap to the sky. Yet even amid those dread, commonplace hours, even during those days when the hard objective world remained apparently intact, a new spirit was upsprouting.

Our information with regard to the first years of the primitive church is extremely scant. Many centuries later when the original ideas of Christianity seemed to be obscured by an extravagant sacerdotal efflorescence earnest attempts were made to discover out of the past the outline of their beginnings. Many simple minds set for themselves the duty of digging down to the original quick seed. It is a task not without pathos and by no means easy of accomplishment. The most diligent investigations are rewarded with little enough, and the hints revealed do not easily fall in with the requirements of a later society. The passing of a very few generations sufficed to show the confusions latent in this religion. The pure teaching of Jesus, as we have already seen, was unadapted to any practical and consistent scheme of living. The miraculous interpretations put upon it rendered its development still more complicated. It was found necessary to accommodate its elusive concepts to those hard facts of the world so scorned by its original founder. This the church, with its long experience, eventually succeeded in doing. It adapted the spirit to the letter, but in achieving this in a large measure it lost sight of the truth in Jesus' words. That pure fountain of living water—who can now trace it back to its source? Each dogma sanctioned has been but an iron nail, an iron nail dangerously capable of rusting. Even after the calamity of the crucifixion the power of Jesus was strong upon His disciples. These fishermen and religious enthusiasts remained still under the glamour of their dead Rab. His spirit could not be put out, no, not by death itself. Somehow or another they came to believe that the end was not yet.

The rumour that He had risen from the dead persisted. A score of years passed by and these strange stories came to be constantly repeated. He had revisited the glimpses of the moon. He had been seen in the day-time, in the night-time. With a body material and at the same time immaterial He had been with His disciples. He had continually appeared amongst them. In the charm of the dawn, before the wild fowl rose from their feeding grounds, He had been visible to them on the shore of the Lake of Galilee. He had suddenly been in the midst of them in their secret assemblies behind thick walls and bolted doors. They had spoken with Him, touched Him, seen Him eat fish and break bread. Then, as the years passed, these imaginings became more and more circumstantial. Simple memories that had to do with the weeks immediately following the crucifixion took to themselves the very quality of poetry. The narration of the meeting on the road to Emmaus could not have been invented. It has about it the true ring of a story spoken with conviction. The cool perceptions of these men had become confused in their overwrought condition. As the years passed the talk of an excited afternoon took permanent shape. The emotion that had evoked it was true. Those apostolic heads were at a loss what to think. "The Lord is risen indeed! . . . and they said one to another, Did not our heart burn within us while He talked with us by the way, and while He opened to us the Scriptures?" Then, as demands for a valid evidence increased, these half-forgotten impressions were written down as facts, impressions of the very kind to gain credence easily enough amongst those whose minds had never been intimidated by the strict instructions of science. It was asserted that after forty days Jesus had led the twelve to Bethany. "And it came to pass, while He blessed them, He was parted from them, and carried up into heaven," or again, "and when He had spoken these things, while they beheld, He was taken up; and a cloud received Him out of their sight." Theologians are content to account for such manifestations by the words "condescensions for evidential purposes." There exist of course a hundred miraculous legends of the same kind in other primitive religions. The use and wont of a provincial and uncritical upbringing incline many of us to accept such devout whim-whams, whereas if they were derived from sources less familiar they would not be received for a single moment. Yet we are safe in asserting that such miraculous claims did very appreciably contribute to the rapid spread of Christianity. Sunday, the day of Mithras, rather than the Sabbath was very early set apart by the faithful in commemoration of the imagined resurrection of Jesus.

For the rest, this insignificant Jewish sect could have hardly been clearly differentiated from any other peculiar Jewish community. They obeyed the law of Moses, attended the temple services, and were satisfied to follow their own particular devotions under the shadow of the ancient religion of their fathers. They believed what the Pharisees believed, except that they cherished the conviction that the master they had loved so much was in very truth the Messiah. They must wait and see in a mood of repentance and righteousness. It was what their nation had been doing for centuries, and they could surely do it for that short interval of time which divided them from the last day when they would see Jesus appear suddenly over Mount Scopus in clouds of glory. During that first decade no one could have predicted the future of the faith. With nothing but a few hallowed memories to maintain its life it surely would be inevitably lost in the tireless drift of time.

CHAPTER V

SAINT PAUL

CHRISTIANITY was saved by the genius of a single man. During the years when Jesus was shaping ox goads at Nazareth, St. Paul had been born at Tarsus. His parents were Jews of the dispersion. They were Hebrews of the Hebrews. The boy apparently very early in life showed a passion for the stiff religion of his race. He was sent to Jerusalem to receive instructions from Gamaliel, the greatest teacher of his age, " held in honour of all the people." Under the guidance of this good, tolerant, and learned man he submitted his youthful and turbulent spirit to the direction of the Torah. For an interval of time his impassioned nature found satisfaction in the strict application of the punctilious injunctions of those traditional codes. He thought by means of an exact obedience to save his soul alive ! Yet such a release could only be for a time. The problem of Saul was the problem of a man spiritually sick. Subject himself as he might to the arbitrary rules of conduct prescribed by his faith his frustrated spirit still thirsted for a deeper and surer peace. To rid himself of his restless torture his fanaticism turned its attention to " the case " of others. The greatest sufferers have always been the greatest persecutors. The damned torture best. It was at this juncture that the young Pharisee came into contact with the primitive Christians who with a harmless devotion were fulfilling as best they might their simple mission. They were convinced that Jesus had risen from the grave and upon the strength of this conviction were confident that their beloved crucified master was shortly to reappear again to inaugurate the Messianic age. This " inside information " they felt it incumbent upon themselves to spread abroad. They therefore went about preaching that Jesus had risen, and called upon men to repent in order that they might be ready for the new order. They concerned themselves with fitting the ancient prophecies to the life of their beloved. Their creed was as simple as it was incredible. It consisted of five articles:

1. Jesus died for our sins.
2. Jesus was buried.
3. Jesus rose from the dead on the third day.
4. Jesus appeared to St. Peter.
5. Jesus appeared to the other disciples.

It is hardly likely that at first they thought of Him as a god. He probably was regarded still in the light of a peculiar messenger. Yet even so the sweet influence they had absorbed enabled these good men to approach life from an entirely new angle. It was as though they had suddenly been permitted to enjoy an unheard-of emancipation. "The peace of God which passeth all understanding" was upon them, and their bigoted compatriots were astonished to observe the " joy in believing " that characterized the new brotherhood. With their mysterious watchword, " Jesus is Lord," upon their lips they went out into the narrow thoroughfares of the doomed city carrying their good tidings. All was different with them now.

They tried to put into practice the explicit teaching they had received. They held their possessions in common. They were filled with brotherly love. In the face of the greatest dangers they manifested an inexplicable cheerfulness, that gladness of mien under persecutions which for many future years was to distinguish members of their faith. They perhaps formed their own small synagogue. They certainly met constantly for a common meal called the "Agape," while the vantage point they selected for public preaching seems to have been Solomon's Porch.

There they were to be heard, these ignorant and unlearned men, so pious, so devout, and so highly to be esteemed, explaining their unreasonable vision of life. Some of the words they spoke during those early days have come down to us. St. Peter, who was used to hold to an oar, who was used to go fishing half naked, who had the good common sense of a plain, rough, fishing-smack fisherman, revealed the astounding fact that he could reason as well as another. In clear words he explained to his audience what had happened. "But Peter, standing up with the eleven, lifted up his voice, and said unto them, . . . Ye men of Israel, hear these words; Jesus of Nazareth, a man approved of God among you by miracles and wonders and signs, which God did by Him in the midst of you, as ye yourselves also know: Him being delivered by the determinate counsel and foreknowledge of God, ye have taken, and by wicked hands have crucified and slain: Whom God hath raised up, having loosed the pains of death: because it was not possible that He should be holden of it . . . this Jesus hath God raised up, whereof we all are witnesses." And there were found others to propound after the manner of the times the plausible sequence of this artless propaganda, and not only to elucidate its significance, but to drive home with shrewd words the disturbing fact that the Jews had, as likely as not, actually executed their long-looked-for Messiah, taking him for a deceiver. " Ye stiffnecked and uncircumcised in heart and ears, ye do always resist the Holy Ghost : as your fathers did, so do ye. Which of the prophets have not your fathers persecuted? And they have slain them which shewed before of the coming of the Just One; of Whom ye have been now the betrayers and murderers." Words of this kind uttered with all the conviction of a youthful convert were insupportable hearing to the young Pharisaic enthusiast, Saul. Those who looked at St. Stephen, " saw his face as it had been the face of an angel." There is no more dangerous emotion than spiritual jealousy, and this now entirely took possession of the future apostle and he acquiesced in, if he did not actively compass, the young man's death. Pontius Pilate had been recalled to Rome and there was probably no authority strong enough to prevent this sinister demonstration of mob violence. St. Stephen lay dead and the garments of the stone-throwers were heaped at the feet of Saul. The persecution of the early Christians had begun.

Still nursing his evil conscience, his uncertainty, and his passionate zeal, Saul set out for Damascus. But before ever he reached that ancient oasis of palm trees and running water his heart was changed. This inhibited man was suddenly convinced that the misguided sect of heretics he hated was offering to the world no lies but truth. We shall never know what he saw or heard on that memorable journey. The ferment of his spirit broke out at last and created a miraculous objective vision. This indeed was the Absolute Love he had been secretly seeking all the time, calling out (through the crack of a man's heart) to Jewish lust-love, hot, human, too human, jealous; and murderous to boot! In a second, in a moment of time, all his suppressions found release. *He was free!*

The real inventor of Christianity as a world religion is not, of course, Jesus Christ at all; but this astounding springal of a Pharisee. Few characters in history have been more baffling; none so furiously hated, none so saturated with paradoxes. One sees him as ugly, with a heart-breaking sort of peculiar ugliness, the psychic distortion of a passionately "pure" sex pervert, whose spirituality is his one escape from incredible temptations. One sees him as the Jew of Jews; as the veritable "wandering Jew" of the spirit. There simmer in him, in this inventor of the religion of Europe and both the Americas, all the monomanias that from Abraham to John the Baptist seethe like the milk of so many devils' dams in Jewish veins. How erudite in the Scriptures he is! Hola! Hela! the great Rabbi! And yet to what a scream of wild banshee-like, werewolf "love" does he tune the dance of his crazy nerves! On the other hand, no man has ever put a firmer thumb down on the hidden foul pustules of mushroom-like evil and made such black juice squirt out. A black magician he was, but Oyez! how he could blow the bugles of the Orphic mystery when he so wantonly willed! Who knew so well, none knew so well, what it is to love till you give your body to be burned, and yet are left in the lurch, and fall short, and cannot quite do it! And who was it but he (Paul commonly called Saul) who found out, through his deep taboos and totems, half Jewish, half God knows what, the world-undermining doctrine about the weak overcoming the strong, the foolish overcoming the clever, the (and here his craziness left that of Jesus Himself behind) things that are not, overcoming the things that are! How extraordinary that it should have been left to this aspiring egoist, "with a heart of furious fancies," to have been caught up into the Third Heaven where he saw things rather to be concealed than to be revealed. Yet it was this man, this prodigious egoist of all complexes, with his enigmatic thorn in the flesh, who in a manner more spiritual than all the twelve disciples, loved the Redeemer of the World. He it was who had the real peculiarity of becoming literally nothing, *le Néant*, in the adoration of what he worshipped so desperately, "and yet not I, but Christ which is in me."

Saint Augustine said somewhere that the church owes Paul to the prayer of Stephen. "*Si Stephanus non orasset Ecclesia Paulum non haberet.*" This is undoubtedly true. "Lord Jesus, receive my spirit . . . Lord, lay not this sin to their charge." Doubt it not, these devout, generous words were lurking at the back of his mind when he called up that vision which led him to realize his true vehicle of expression. St. Paul took the religion of the early Christians with its simple faith in the Messiah and lifted it into the realm of high mystical import. Jesus became the Christ indeed. Through faith, and by means of the sacraments, it was possible, so Paul now taught, for any individual to put himself into direct spiritual contact with this new God. It was in this way that he solved his own problem, thereby finding a solution for the unhappiness of others. He it was who presented the new religion and launched it down the ages. He had small culture. The wisdom of the Greeks was nothing to him, the most beautiful works of art nothing. He held that the particular mystical ecstasy which he daily experienced was alone of real consequence. And, suddenly, out of the mouth of this ugly Jew who laid his hand so heavily upon the heads of all women to keep 'em quiet, to keep 'em down, there issued the strangest and wildest and most beautiful of love songs. It was as though a toad sitting under a burdock leaf had suddenly opened its wide gaping mouth and lo! because there was love in its heart had been able to give utterance to a music more beautiful than the singing of any hermit-thrush. We have here the cry of a lover captive and passionate. This is a new voice breaking the stillness of our night. Say what we will, with these words something fresh came into the world. "Charity suffereth long, and is kind; charity envieth not; charity vaunteth not itself; is not puffed up . . . Beareth all things, believeth all things, hopeth all things, endureth all things."

This, then, in a word was the achievement of St. Paul. He took from St. Peter the simplicities of the faith and converted them into a reasonable, unreasonable ecstasy adapted to the needs of the human heart. He separated Christianity from its socket of narrow close-fitting Judaism and made it possible for all men to have a share in the new religion; and yet at the same time his peculiar education enabled him to take advantage of the age-long Hebrew intuition in matters of religion. His theology was essentially the theology of his upbringing, but with something added; and that something was everything, was indeed the idea *of the living Christ.* St. Paul knew how to weave material tents under which travellers could shelter their bodies from the sun and the rain of the real world; he knew also how to weave a pavilion destined for two thousand years to serve as a protection for men's souls. To be soothed, to be saved by faith in Christ, that was the boon he offered. The historical figure of Jesus meant little to him, the historical simulacrum of that man who had gone to and fro over the curtailed, dusty, bleached slopes of Palestine. Jesus was dead and buried; but through St. Paul's personal revelations, and through his daily experience of an unaccountable bliss, Christ was enthroned. It was in the love of Christ that he lived and moved and had his being. Nothing else mattered to him. The superb statues of Athens were to him naught but so many idols; the subtleties of Greek thought but a "show of wisdom"; all the magical mystery of the insurgent natural world was nothing and less than nothing. He had become a bondslave to Christ; the gift of the grace and of the spirit of Christ was to St. Paul all in all.

When one contemplates the large measure of folly ever present in us men, with skulls empty as pots, our ignorance of our emotional possibilities, our disposition to follow any persuasive suggestion without prevision or reflection, we can hardly be surprised that when once the idea of our redemption by Jesus had been plausibly put, many were converted. The submerged population, half educated and given over to superstition, listened with easy and enthusiastic attention to this new creed that promised salvation on such easy terms. In those days the dreams and prophecies of even the youngest converts made it constantly evident that "the Holy Ghost was present."

Here were joyful tidings, and tidings that found convincing proof in the singular possession given to the faithful as "powers of the coming age." For it must be remembered that these early Christians were taught to believe in the speedy coming of Jesus. It was an illusion that must always be reckoned with. St. Paul's own opinion on this matter is evident from the following quotations: "And that, knowing the time, that now it is high time to awake out of sleep: for now is our salvation nearer than when we believed" (Rom. xiii. 11). "For our conversation is in heaven; from whence also we look for the Saviour, the Lord Jesus Christ" (Phil. iii. 20). "But of the times and the seasons, brethren, ye have no need that I write unto you. For yourselves know perfectly that the day of the Lord so cometh as a thief in the night. For when they shall say, Peace and safety; then sudden destruction cometh upon them, as travail upon a woman with child; and they shall not escape. But ye, brethren, are not in darkness, that that day should overtake you as a thief" (1 Thess. v. 1–4).

Such then was the teaching that under his guidance and direction spread itself abroad from Antioch to Alexandria, from Alexandria to Rome. His wider conception of the faith was at first vigorously resisted by those who had known Jesus personally. "But when Peter was come to Antioch, I withstood him to the face, because he was to be blamed." Presently, however, they too suppressed their memories and sure knowledge and were swept forward on the wave of St. Paul's zeal. Just as a single seed adhering to the leather of the sole of a bird's foot may spread the hosts of a new flower over a wide land, so now did this one man spread forth his message.

It is curious to meditate upon that passage in the New Testament which contains the first reference that we possess to the belief that a Syrian workman was actually the son of God. Little wonder that so startling a claim should have kept the theologians occupied for so many generations. The first mention of Jesus Christ in the literature of the human race is contained in one of St. Paul's epistles. To apprehend the true significance of this script the mind should be allowed to forget for a moment all the ancient religious cults of Babylon, of Egypt, and of Greece, and to imagine man as a "wise ape" gradually acquiring the arts of civilization, learning to tame beasts, learning to develop corn out of grass, learning to live with others of his kind in hand-built habitations. With labour, with fury, with bloodshed, men established themselves in cities, until an occasion could arise when an inspired tentmaker at Corinth filled with an unreasoning love could boldly assert that one of their number, who, while he lived, had been invisible to sight from the distance of a mile, was in very truth a God. The letter was carried to Thessalonica, a free commercial Greek city that took its name from the sister of Alexander the Great.

The black tree-trunk gods of Africa, the frantic antic deities of America, the gods of the Nile valley, Marduk, Moloch, Apollo, and Pan himself had now taken a new incarnation, strange and neurotic. The pain, the unhappiness, the deep sorrow abroad in the world, had created the need for a new worship, and a certain mysterious figure who, in a profound manner, fulfilled this unconscious desire had lived and died *and had been remembered.* What a novel timbre is touched in the New Testament style! Here is a violin the taut strings of which are made of no common cat's gut. "Paul, and Silvanus, and Timotheus, unto the church of the Thessalonians which is in God the Father and in the Lord Jesus Christ: Grace be unto you, and peace, from God our Father, and the Lord Jesus Christ. We give thanks to God always for you all, making mention of you in our prayers; Remembering without ceasing your work of faith, and labour of love, and patience of hope in our Lord Jesus Christ, in the sight of God and our Father; knowing, brethren beloved, your election of God. For our gospel came not unto you in word only, but also in power, and in the Holy Ghost, and in much assurance; as ye know what manner of men we were among you for your sake. And ye became followers of us, and of the Lord, having received the word in much affliction, with joy of the Holy Ghost: So that ye were ensamples to all that believe in Macedonia and Achaia. For from you sounded out the word of the Lord, not only in Macedonia and Achaia, but also in every place your faith to God-ward is spread abroad; so that we need not to speak anything. For they themselves show of us what manner of entering in we had unto you, and how ye turned to God from idols to serve the living and true God; And to wait for His Son from heaven, whom He raised from the dead, even Jesus, which delivered us from the wrath to come."

CHAPTER VI

THE SPREADING OF CHRISTIANITY

THE new religion with its universal appeal spread rapidly from city to city. Churches were formed, the congregations of which spoke apocalyptic words. Oppressed, ignorant, and spiritually hungry, they threw themselves enthusiastically into the new movement. The rumour was whispered abroad everywhere. A new God had risen from the dead and His supernatural living presence in the world could be recognized by anyone who had the confidence to believe in Him. The Parousia was at hand. It remained only to fulfil the new doctrine of personal purity and of service to others, and to turn to God from idols and " to wait for His Son from heaven whom He raised from the dead, even Jesus, which delivered us from the wrath to come."

St. Paul eventually found his way to Rome, but long before he reached the great capital the new religion had been established there. The Pagan world of Rome walking at ease backwards and forwards from its shrines and temples, meditating at ease in its cool porticoes or being borne in litters along its great world roads, became more and more often aware of the new and unfamiliar religious movement. Suetonius records that the Emperor Claudius " banished from Rome the Jews who made great tumult because of Chrestus" (*Judæos impulsore Chresto assidue tumultuantes Roma expulit*). With this sentence in mind we are justified in concluding that within fifteen or twenty years of the crucifixion the dissensions amongst the Jewish communities at Rome, in consequence of the rise of Christianity, were important enough to provoke government interference. Tacitus also has left us reliable evidence in support of the Christian tradition with regard to the persecutions of the disturbing sect by order of Nero. He refers to the "Christiani" with open antipathy, and explains that they derive their name from "Christus" who was "condemned to death in the reign of Tiberius by the Procurator Pontius Pilate." We also have the celebrated letter written by Pliny the younger to Trajan proving that the Christians were accustomed to collect together in his province of Bithynia to sing sacred songs appealing to "Christus" as God. Lastly, we have the fragment in *The Antiquities* of Josephus which, although it would seem to have undergone certain interpolations at the hands of Christians anxious to strengthen the evidence as to the early importance of the faith, again goes to prove that the new religion was well known to the cultured world at the end of the first century. These famous allusions to Christianity form the somewhat thin classical background for the story of the beginning of the religion. It is curious in these latter days how it has been the custom to argue this way and that from these slender references. A few accidental words preserved out of the past take to themselves a huge significance for some, while others are inclined to doubt that Jesus ever existed. It is a matter to be decided by the taste and temperament of each individual. The origin of this consolation, the hidden, absolute origin of it, is, we suspect, far different from our imaginings, whether we be heathen or Christian. All is obscured in the dim mists of a forgotten past. However, " if the lion skin be not large enough we must e'en make it up with a scantling of foxes."

We are fortunate in having in our possession the early Christian versions of these happenings. The tradition of the persecutions under Nero which the Christians have handed down may probably be relied upon. In all likelihood it was under the rule of Nero that St. Peter met his death, but whether his faithful, aged bones were used as a torch to illumine the emperor's garden, or whether he was actually crucified head downwards, is a question the truth of which we can now never hope to know. It is clear that a great movement was in progress, a kind of surging under-current was everywhere making itself felt. A new doctrine was spreading, spreading, spreading; a new doctrine that had life in it, a life that refused to be killed. These tent-makers, tax-gatherers, physicians, artisans, and slaves, these women and children, had come in touch with a secret that ignored entirely the accepted standards of Rome. Ignorant of, or in-different to, intelligent evaluations of the human situation they relied upon their own emotional clue, their own curious " illative sense." As the existence of this new superstition disclosed itself efforts were made to suppress it. *Christiani non sint* (Christians must not exist). But behold, these efforts which, although intermittent were often vigorous enough, encountered an unheard-of resistance. The survival of Christianity can undoubtedly be explained to a very large extent by the " cloud of witnesses " which everywhere arose. These men, women, and children were at any moment prepared to face death in its most horrible form for the sake of their new madness. Their irrational conduct was from the first irritating to the philosophic mind. "The readiness for death must proceed from inward conviction, not come of mere perversity like the Christians," wrote Marcus Aurelius; while Gibbon annotates the phenomenon with the following scoffing commentary: "The ancient Christians were animated by a contempt for their present existence, and by a just confidence of immortality, of which the doubtful and imperfect faith of modern ages cannot give us any adequate notion." The Pagan world was duly impressed. If men were prepared to outface the common dread at this rate an uncommon virtue must be contained in their belief. No one can do more than lay down his life for a cause. The seeds of this harvest-field were drops of blood. The fickle populations, their minds debased by the grosser practices of the heathen world, went trooping off to watch the sports in the amphitheatres, and behold! there they saw a band of feeble Christians displaying a gladness in death of some inexplicable engendering beyond anything within the experience of these casual spectators. "Perpetua followed with shining steps . . . as the darling of God, abashing with the high spirit in her eyes the gaze of all." Agathonica leaped into flames crying, "Lord Lord, Lord help me, for I flee unto thee." "I am a Christian and nothing evil is done amongst us," calls out Blandina in her extremity. There can be no smoke without fire, and it became more and more evident that these degenerates were not fooling. A new thing was out in the streets that had to be dealt with. It grew apace. What was this rumour that came seeping through everywhere into the rational ways of life? It was openly declared before the seat of judgment in the Roman court. It was whispered into the ears of the frivolous Roman matron by the slave girl who was tiring her hair. The very chains of the Christians "were worn by them as a comely ornament . . . exhaling at the same time the sweet savour of Christ so that some thought they had been anointed with perfume of this world." A simple explanation of all the bewildering mystery had been found, a sure and certain explanation the truth of which could be easily tested.

What a glimpse into the early days of this religion is given by a visit to the catacombs of Rome! These passages, long enough if placed end to end to reach from the Appian Way to Warmwell Cross Roads, are eloquent of the incipient hours of this fantasy. With their illiterate, unclassical, cryptographic lithographs these inspired millions lived like rats with shining eyes underground. To look at their inscriptions on the cold tufa, to observe their occult symbols of hope, their anchors and their fish, marked out so scrupulously; to weary oneself in counting their martyrs' tombs, to see their bones at rest in their shelves after so many hundreds of years, offers a most liberal instruction. There is something disconcerting about visiting these darkened tunnels of an ancient illusion that have at no time received the blessing of the sun. These men who lived like rats, like the ubiquitous brown rat, came up out of their passages to populate the cities. No cranny too small for them to squeeze through, no plank too narrow for their feet to tread! Fire. water, poison, stones, hedge sticks, nothing availed to stamp their breed out. Up from their catacombs they came and converted the world. I recollect that I saw some black hair adhering still to one of those exposed skulls, and the look of its matted texture, so dusty and yet of so lively a colour, shocked my imagination into a vivid understanding of the amazing achievement of these enthusiasts whose heads had whirled so wildly with misinformation. Who can tell how they did it? but somehow they managed to convert the heathen world. To go down into those pits where so many of the deluded dead lie "free" in their galleries, to go down into them from out of the disobedient sunshine is stimulating to the mind of a man. By means of such an excursion fresh insights are gained. The importunate, everyday life of our own moment of time, with the Colosseum and the Baths of Caracalla still standing, falls back into a due perspective. The cold, patient, unstipulating walls of these "dug-outs" become articulate. It is all but impossible to accustom our minds to a full comprehension of humanity's frenzied gift of self-deception. Nothing on the surface abides, nothing is constant. All is carried forward upon a stream of change. Below the sullen actuality of matter, below the balanced, suspended, floating thoughts of human speculation, below the involved solutions of our spiritual dilemmas, lies a poetry utterly void of participation. It is a poetry without end or beginning. It is a poetry without morality or immorality. The invisible thread of a harebell's stalk quivers with it, and at its purposeless behest the mighty constellations gather to their folds in the night sky. Its manifestations are many. It experiments without cessation. Mindful and unmindful of human fortune it would as lief create an inquisitor as a Jesus. "Wake up and dream!" What a phenomenon of phenomena was this phantasmagoria of the spirit which for two thousand years was destined to cloud men's minds. The secret of Jesus was true and holy, His genius offered a lofty lesson, but it was incompatible with the indurate manners of the world. In spite of all the chicanery of the church it has lived on, its power remaining fresh and unabated for many centuries: it survives still in the hearts of some very simple and very rare people.

CHAPTER VII

AN HISTORICAL APOSTOLIC SUCCESSION

It is not, perhaps, from the church at Rome that it is easiest to trace the direct tradition of that apostolic succession which connects primitive Christianity with the disciples of Jesus. We must go to Asia Minor to do this. The names that form the bridge are those of John the Evangelist; Polycarp, Bishop of Smyrna; Papias, Bishop of Hierapolis; and Irenæus, Bishop of Lyons. From Christian traditions that can hardly be challenged it seems that St. John, the Divine, who because of his zealotry had been playfully named by Jesus the son of thunder, lived to a very great age, dying indeed in the reign of Trajan. Although there may be some confusion with another John it seems reasonable to believe that the beloved disciple spent the last years of his life at Ephesus, having under his direction the seven churches of Asia. As the years passed his character seems to have undergone a change. An attractive legend relates that the aged disciple was observed one day tenderly carrying a partridge in his hands. Those who ministered to him boldly inquired how it came about that he cherished this small bird with its soft barred feathers: whereat the old man answered that the whole teaching of Jesus sprang from, and was centred about, the single word *love*.

Irenæus, the Bishop of Lyons, who was born about A.D. 130, records that Polycarp in early life "had been taught by apostles and lived in familiar intercourse with many that had seen Christ." He writes also these remarkable words to a certain Florinus: "I saw thee when I was still a boy in lower Asia in company with Polycarp . . . I can even now point out the place where the blessed Polycarp used to sit when he discoursed, and describe his goings out and comings in, his manner of life, and his personal appearance, and the discourses which he delivered to the people, how he used to speak of his intercourse with John and with the rest of those who had seen the Lord, and how he would relate their words. And everything that he had heard from them about the Lord, about His miracles, and about His teaching, Polycarp used to tell us as one who had received it from them who had seen the Word of Life with their own eyes, and all this in perfect harmony with the Scriptures. To these things I used to listen at the time, through the mercy of God vouchsafed to me, noting them down, not on paper but in my heart, and constantly by the grace of God I brood over my accurate recollections." It is to be noticed that Papias, who was also "a companion of Polycarp," used to assert that he put more reliance upon such oral tradition than upon written documents, of which he expresses a somewhat contemptuous opinion. It was perhaps for this very reason that Eusebius of Cæsarea describes Papias as a man of small mental capacity "who took the figurative language of apostolic tradition for actual fact."

It is certainly of extraordinary interest to us to think that these old men of the old times were actually privileged to listen to the talk of Polycarp, who had heard from the lips of St. John a hundred stories of what Jesus said and did which were never "put down": memories that had to do perhaps with John's good father, the aged Zebedee, or with the characteristics of those hired servants we read about in the gospels, or how the man who cast out devils in the name of Jesus had looked; where exactly he had been met with, standing in the centre of an interested group on some road indented with camels' feet, or near some village well where fig trees flourished. Polycarp must have heard also of the raising of Lazarus, and of St. Paul's visit to Jerusalem after his first missionary journey. Polycarp was and is a most celebrated pillar of the church, and we are in a position to give a good deal of historical information about his life, a fact which renders his connexion with St. John of priceless value.

According to Tertullian he was appointed to his position as Bishop of Smyrna by the apostle. He was probably born a year or two before the destruction of Jerusalem and we know that he was put to death in A.D. 155. "His influence was that of saintliness rather than that of intellect." We know little about his life at Smyrna; between the years of 115 and 155 practically nothing. Ignatius, when on his way to suffer martyrdom at Rome, stayed in his house. We conclude from a letter that Ignatius wrote at the time that he must have been an excitable kind of guest for Polycarp to have entertained. "Now I begin to be a disciple. Fire and cross, troops of wild beasts, rending of every limb, dire torments of the devil let them come to me, if only I may follow Jesus Christ . . . I am God's wheat, and I am ground by the teeth of wild-beasts that I may be found Christ's pure bread." Polycarp was a stout opponent of heresy. "For every one who shall not confess that Jesus Christ is come in the flesh is antichrist; and whosoever shall not confess the testimony of the cross is damned." Shortly before his death Polycarp visited Rome to consult with the bishop Anicetus of church matters. It was here that he met with the heretic Marcion, who accosted the old man with the appeal, "Recognize us," and was received for his pains with the churlish rebuff, "I recognize you as the first born of Satan." Perhaps it was the rise of the ethico-dualistic religion of that reformer which caused Polycarp in the last years of his life constantly to cry out, "Oh good God, to what times thou hast spared me, that I must suffer such things," an exclamation which has been echoed by many another dogma-ridden churchman down through the ages.

The noblest glimpse we have of Polycarp has to do with his tragic end. In his eighty-sixth year a great Pagan festival took place in Smyrna and the excited populace raised a cry against the bishop. "Away with the atheist. Let search be made for Polycarp. . . . This is the teacher of Asia, the father of the Christians, the destroyer of our gods, who teaches many not to sacrifice or worship. . . . *Let loose the lion on Polycarp*." He was brought back to the city from a farm to which he had retired. In a letter written to the Church of God we may read what happened. It is a record of poignant realism. The governor took Polycarp up into his chariot and tried to persuade him to make some reasonable concessions. The old man proved obdurate, however, and was hustled so roughly out of the conveyance that he hurt his shin. "He, as though nothing had happened, paid no heed, but went on quickly with much eagerness on his way to the stadium, where the din was so great that none could be so much as heard." The Proconsul now demanded that he should "curse Christ." It was then that the aged priest uttered those proud words, so full of beauty and dignity. "Eighty and six years have I served Him, and He did me no wrong. How can I blaspheme my King, that saved me?" It was observed that the Jews were especially active in preparing the fuel that was to burn him to death. Before a man could wink these agile sons of Belial had gathered from their shops sufficient timber for their purpose. They bound him to the stake, and "the fire forming a sort of arch, like a ship's sail bellying with the wind, made a wall about the body of the martyr, which was in the midst, not like burning flesh, but like bread in the baking." Even when it was over no one was allowed to approach the charred remains of the saint lest "the Christians would now forsake the crucified and worship Polycarp." However, in spite of the centurion set to watch the place of execution, those devoted to him did manage to take away some of his ashes "of more value than precious stones."

CHAPTER VIII

GNOSTICISM AND THE DOCTRINE OF MARCION

We have seen how Polycarp put Marcion into his place, and it may be well just here to say a few words about this celebrated heretic. He was a rich ship-owner belonging to Sinope in Pontus. It was reported that he had been cast out of the church for seducing a virgin. Whether or not this accusation was true the man appeared suddenly in Rome with his head full of theological theories and cherishing the conviction that he, after St. Paul, had been raised up to proclaim the true gospel. His purpose was identical with that of many later-day reformers. He deeply suspected the embryonic Catholic church. Much of its teaching appeared to him both shallow and inconsistent. Like many another he had a mind to rebuild religion upon the actual words of Jesus as they were to be found in the " authentic " gospel, and as they had been interpreted by St. Paul. In his view the orthodox Christian doctrines offered to the world *had already been corrupted*. It was not the pure word as it had been revealed. He was a dualist yet he was not a thorough-going Gnostic, for he steadfastly held to the opinion that salvation was to be won not through " knowledge," but through faith in those divine secrets revealed to mankind through Christ.

But the secret of Jesus in actual fact can never be

recaptured. It never has existed in any ultimate rational form. It is intangible as the breath of a child in sleep, delicate and insubstantial as a tear. It is inexplicable as a blessing, and particular and universal as summer grass. There is everything and nothing in it. If a scribe had been standing by, scroll in hand to take down the actual words Jesus spoke, still no logical theology could be made out of them. His personality has bewitched men, filled their wits with a new moon-madness, but from the first moment that men tried to put the emotion that they felt into reasonable language they of necessity began to create error. As there was no foundation for any theory, all theories were possible, and in consequence we see the field of thought prepared for the endless theological discussions that have exercised the ingenuity of the religious for twenty centuries. Below theology, and indeed below all metaphysical speculation, lies a vast surging ocean of mystery that can throw up and take back to itself a thousand spray clouds of varied rainbow colour.

Marcion was quick to see that the God of the Old Testament had a very different disposition from the God of the New Testament. He reconciled them in this way: Jehovah was a rough rude Demiurge who had created men and then put them all under a curse because of their inability to keep his law. Another god, of whose existence Jehovah was ignorant, took pity on men and sent down his only son to save them. Jehovah never suspected who he was and caused him to be hanged on the cross. Overawed by Christ's appearance in glory, and by a certain misgiving that he had acted against the spirit of his own law, Jehovah promised to deliver up the souls of those who were to be saved to this good unknown god, they having been purchased from him by the death of Christ. This was the basic idea of his new church which grew rapidly in importance and survived for several generations. Marcion's theories were not exactly philosophical, they were the product of a practical mind which found the greatest difficulty in reconciling the Christian concept with the crude ideas out of which it had sprung. He is always occupied with detailed and unrewarding reconciliations and quaint overstrained consistencies. For example, he taught that when Christ (with the mandate wrested from Jehovah) proceeded to the underworld to rescue the souls of the dead, only the more wayward of the old Hebrew heroes responded to His call, men like Cain, Esau, and the unfortunate Saul: the prophets being content to remain in Abraham's bosom, having been tricked, as Marcion explained, too often by their God to be lightly deceived by the hearsay of any cosmological transaction as hard to comprehend as the atonement.

What was really happening to the central body of Christian fellowship? "Everywhere there was readiness to experiment, and where circumstances seemed to demand it, to change." There was a danger in this state of things. Obviously, without authority and dogma "the prevailing party" could never hope to prosper. Christianity offered a supernatural explanation, and for this very reason it could admit of no discrepancies of belief. When doctrines that are unproven and unprovable are put forward in the guise of absolute truth it is the solid consensus of opinion that ultimately counts. From the earliest times those who directed church affairs realized the advantage to be derived from majority thought.

They realize it to-day. At first, however, there were several rival schools of theology often promoted by men whose mental integrity was to them of far more consequence than any worldly consideration. A hard matter it is to trace the slow development of Catholic teaching. The Church was like some enormous octopus with long trailing feelers; its wavering abdomen kept assimilating and rejecting, assimilating and rejecting, year after year. From the first it was nourished with truth and falsehood. It combined the growth and life of the spirit with the mortmain of worldliness. If it was to survive at all it must conform, it must make concessions.

The Græco-Roman world of the first and second centuries was waiting for such adjustments. Everywhere an interest in matters of religion was being shown. In many cases the old formal traditional worship of Athens and Rome was giving place to novel cults that made a more direct appeal to those mystical inclinations latent in all men. It was expedient for the Church, nay, necessary for her to draw sustenance from these. But not only had she to adapt herself to the emotional requirements of the age, but to the intellectual requirements also. The rabble might be satisfied with religious experience unsupported by metaphysical reasoning, but not so the educated classes. The childish story that the church had to relate must at all costs be given an intellectual formula plausible enough to content the most exacting philomath. The first of these two reconciliations was effected by the sacraments, the second by means of writings such as the fourth gospel, the deliberate object of which was to show that the idea of Christianity was by no means incompatible with Platonic speculation. As the ages passed Christianity gathered to itself every chance straw from the four quarters of the wind and soberly set about to thatch a water-tight roof as a permanent shelter for its members. Years passed by. Winds blew away large portions of it, moss flourished upon it, starlings and hedge-sparrows nested in it, rats came out of the cellarage and burrowed through it, but still, even to this day, it offers protection to a society of conspirators, obstinate and militant. The very organization of the Roman Empire the church appropriated. It built itself upon its model and by this strength still lives. The church possesses and has always possessed a peculiar cunning of its own. It has moved over the world with the silence and the craft of a serpent. Its head has been up, its viper's eye open, but its belly has never left the ground. The heretical views of Marcion were largely derived from the mythological thought of the Gnostics. This great syncretic mystical religion had a very large influence upon Christianity. " Gnosticism tried to stifle Christianity by embracing it." These two systems, both of which entertained the conception of the salvation of the individual soul, were mutually attractive and repellent to each other, the first owing its origin to myth, and the second to traditional history. The doctrines of Gnosticism were dualistic, having for their seed-idea the struggle between darkness and light as it had been envisaged by the Persians. This Oriental conviction had developed very strangely. Its prevailing ideas had been deeply influenced by contact with Babylonian mystery and Platonism. A vast struggle was for ever taking place between inert matter and the clear light of the spirit. For a soul to be saved it was necessary for a man to be master of a certain charmed knowledge which would make easy for him the passage from this world to the next. To know the names of baleful influences was indeed essential to salvation. It was even asserted that Jesus Himself had learned these sacred words, so that when He descended into hell He might pass freely through the haunted area. The Gnostic mysteries were far older than those of Christianity. They were a product of the fantastic imaginings of the East. The conquests of Alexander had spread them broadcast. In one form or the other they appeared in every corner of the Empire. Gnosticism, in truth, was a deep repository of memories, a reservoir of human myths. It told of fallen deities who had sunk down into the world of matter. It told of primal man, of the "son of man" who had been created to crawl like a worm until the breath of life had been breathed into him by God. It told of the great mother Goddess who came down to the world to render man impotent by an excess of sexual licence, thereby to prevent propagation and the promulgation of further evil. This idea is lurking in the Pagan legend which tells how Astarte herself lived for ten years in the streets of Tyre as a common harlot, and reappears again in the myth of Simon meeting Helena in a brothel of that city.

We must always bear in mind that Christianity appeared when Gnostic reasoning in one form or another was widely established; but Gnostic thought was an aggregate with uncertain definitions, and the newer faith with its narrower doctrines rifled it of its open secrets and continued on its way victorious. The Gnostics tried vainly to do the same. They made a deliberate attempt to assimilate into their broader system the historical figure of Jesus, even going so far as to declare that they were in possession of authentic religious information handed down to them through a pure channel, or secret tradition, from the Saviour Himself. This holy information they endeavoured to take up into their more elaborate design of Persian cosmology, trusting thereby to increase the power of their sacramental magic. For it is to the Gnostics that Christianity owes a whole mass of sacramental mystical ideas.

It would have been a difficult matter for anyone living in those early days to have predicted correctly the future of each of the various sects that ministered to the religious feelings of the time. The political unity of so many different countries offered a brave nursery garden for the cultivation of creeds old and new. The stamp of Roman materialism with the emphasis it laid upon the coarser pleasures of the senses encouraged men to look for less obvious satisfactions. It has always been thus, reaction succeeds reaction. No sooner are we satiated with honey in the comb than we begin to look about askance. A sick conscience follows a sick belly. We lose our taste for the positive pleasures of the sun and are off to look for shade in the corridors of the occult.

One of the religions closely allied to Gnosticism was the worship of Mithras, the Persian sun deity. I have seen a cave in Capri dedicated to this cult. At dawn the fresh light penetrates far into its darkened recesses, but in the afternoon, when all is still, the grot is redolent of shadows. The worship of Mithras and the worship of Jesus closely resembled each other. We know from St. Paul's admonitions that the love feasts of the primitive Christians often degenerated into fellowships of indecorum, and with these others it was not otherwise. The worshippers of Mithras possessed a eucharistic ceremony wherein bread and wine were partaken. They also used bell and candle and holy water. The narrower and more constant Christian tradition proved, however, eventually too strong for this worship. With the recognition of Christianity as the religion of the State the hold of Mithraism on the population grew weaker and weaker, until along with other similar floating fancies it was entirely superseded. Yet curiously enough there has survived, even to our own time, a Gnostic faith. It is to be found amongst the Mandæans who to-day live in the marsh lands of south Babylonia and are authentic representatives of this ancient, mysterious, and overlaid teaching.

CHAPTER IX

PRIMITIVE CHURCH WRITERS

THE epistles of St. Paul and the religious writings that belonged to the apostolic age were succeeded by early apologetics for Christianity. Perhaps the most interesting of these were composed by St. Justin, the martyr. He wrote in the first half of the second century, and in his pages are to be found the best account that we have of the life and religious practices of the primitive Christians. He was born in Samaria and in his youth is said to have handled ploughs that had been made by Jesus. He possessed a philosophic, childish mind. One is continually amazed in reading his work at the brilliance of his miscalculations. He lays especial store on the prophetic writings of the Old Testament, and his collection of apt allusions illustrates to a point of wonder how, when any particular thesis has been accepted, all words can be brought to its service; are, indeed, at its service. He had been converted by seeing the Christians go gladly to their death. "I believe that man who is ready to have his throat cut in testimony of what he says," remarked Pascal, and Justin Martyr was no wiser. He argued, and not, I think, in this case without good sense, that free, happy, careless lovers of life would on no account be so easily reconciled to death as were the early Christians. " For I myself, when I took pleasure in the doctrines of Plato, and heard the Christians slandered, seeing them to be fearless of death and of everything else that was thought dreadful, considered that it was impossible that they should live in wickedness or sensuality: for, who that was a sensualist or licentious, and thought human flesh to be good food, would welcome death that he might be deprived of his enjoyments?" He was strong for "the faith that had once for all been delivered to the saints," and he hotly resented the suggestion so persistently put forward by the heathen, that what the Christians said about the wicked being punished in eternal fire was "a mere boast and a bugbear." He was always ready with an answer. He knew just what to retort when Pagans, teased out of mind by his crazy controversies, said to him, "do ye all then destroy yourselves, and go at once to your God, and give us no further trouble!" He is the great Brother Positive ready for all. Unfortunately his refutation of the Marcion heresy has been lost, but we have several passages to show how antipathetic to him were the ideas of the theological-minded shipbuilder. "And there is a Marcion of Pontus, who is even now teaching his disciples to believe in another and greater god than the Creator. He, by the assistance of devils, has made many of every nation utter blasphemies, denying the Creator of this universe to be God, and causing them to confess another, who as being a greater god has done greater things than He." During one of Saint Justin's travels he was accosted in Ephesus by the Jew Trypho, a learned Rabbi, who had lately escaped from the persecutions in Palestine which had followed the uprisings of the false Messiah, Barcochebas. The dialogue that took place between the two is extant. They parted on the best of terms in the end in spite of certain sharp passages. "But you Christians have all received an idle report, and have formed a Christ for yourselves for whose sake you inconsiderately throw away your lives." The Jew's plain speaking was evidently more irritating to the Christian philosopher than he would have cared openly to confess. "I know not how you can accuse others of being lovers of contention, whilst you have so often shown yourself to be such in this discussion, frequently contradicting what you had previously assented to. 'Because,' said Trypho with grave candour, 'you undertake to prove a thing which is incredible and almost impossible, that God condescended to be born, and to be made man.'"

Perhaps the greatest of all the primitive church writers was Tertullian. He was born at Carthage when Justin Martyr was an old man and lived into the third century. He was a writer of great scholarship and possessed a red-hot spirit. He had gone to Rome to learn the lawyer's trade, and it was there that he was converted to Christianity. With a wide knowledge of the classical writers he was admirably fitted, after making a careful study of the Bible and the sacred church writings, to attack and confute not only Gnosticism, but all the other allied heresies that were just then appearing. His work was truculent. He may be represented as a stinging bee set to guard the entrance of the hive against the intrusion of gnats and drones. He gave the industrious workers within, time to consolidate their intricate manipulations. And then towards the end of his life a most unexpected thing happened. He abandoned his post.

We remember how in Phrygia Minerva gave over her attempt to play upon the flute because her essays with the instrument seemed to disfigure her beautiful lips and how her pipes were picked up by the unfortunate Marsyas, who learnt to bewitch all listeners with the music that he made. In the history of the church much the same thing happened, for suddenly in far Phrygia there arose a man named Montanus who declared himself to be possessed by the Paraclete. The church was still in its infancy when this took place. The force of the apostolic succession was tentatively recognized only, for in Asia, in Syria, in Africa, during the beginning of the Christian era, the system of government " varied from church to church and in the same church at different times." Christianity was still malleable and its organization loose. It was under such conditions that these disturbing prophetic voices were heard. Montanus was not alone in possession of the divine spirit. Two women, Prisca and Maximilla, also believed themselves to be possessed in the same way. The dangers of such pretensions were instinctively recognized by the church fathers. Such fresh " outpourings " of the spirit seemed inopportune. They had taken for granted that the charmed circle of heavenly revelation had been finally closed, and it was they, and they alone, who had been commissioned to preserve its treasures, to preserve them intact as they were and hand them down to future generations. That certain religious souls have been allowed to return to the original fountain out of which all religions spring has always exasperated ecclesiastical minds. The very existence of the church demands that there should be one revelation and not many revelations, one voice and not many voices. All is uncertainty and derangement unless an appeal can be made to a single consistent authority. It is for this reason that the church has always been opposed to the individual revelations of pure souls. In its ultimate essence every form of dogmatic faith is exclusive and aggressive. The power that it has is the measure of the harm it can do. It is not to-day, and it never has been, given to the human race to gain possession of absolute truth. Every creed is rooted in emotion. Life can only be saddled with unwarranted conceits by means of bit and spur. Here is a wild ass that kicks and which inevitably in the end will return to its own place, there to snuff up the winds of nature at its pleasure. The claims of these Kataphrygians were extremely disturbing to the primitive church, which was at that time blindly feeling for its most perfect expression. Certain bishops were unwise enough to arrange for a public disputation with the two frenzied women, and behold! forthwith the bishops were reduced to silence, a humiliating issue long remembered against them in Asia Minor. No reformed church, no man with Puritan sympathies, can read with indifference of this small persecuted band who so stoutly registered their protest at the very outset of the great Catholic procession. They saw these priests gathering together with their flags and banners and regulated liturgies, and knew that the way they were about to take down the broad way of Vanity Fair was not the quiet hedgerow path that had been known to Jesus. The Montanists insisted that a spontaneous return to the teaching of Jesus was essential. They required stricter rules of chastity. In every incident of daily life they wished for a more rigid profession of Christianity, an entire separation from the world and its ways. Not so with the bishops. These pontiffs had already grown accustomed to power and their hearts were now set upon conquering the Western world. Just as St. Paul had made it easy for the Gentiles over the matter of circumcision, so were these men averse to the laying of puritanical burdens upon their unversed congregations. The Montanists claimed that the policy of the Christian fellowship should to a large extent be directed by " the organs of the spirit "; the bishops, on the other hand, were determined to enforce their wishes by a system of ecclesiastical discipline.

The protest of the Montanists marks the epoch in the history of Christianity when the instinct of the church, under pressure of circumstance, and in response to its desire for power, embarked upon secular manners. No longer was it to be a society of religious devotees shut away and opposed to the world. From henceforth it aspired to reconciliations. It went to school at the world university and proved a promising pupil. It matriculated, it took its degree with honours. It was made the Master of Corpus at Rome. It is a memorable fact, and one not to be forgotten, that the greatest of all the great Latin controversialists of early Christianity gave his personal testimony to the validity of the Montanist misgiving by formally leaving the Catholic Church. No one was better versed than Tertullian in the disputes of his time, no one was a greater authority upon the doctrines and purport of Christianity, yet this man, the experience of years upon him, with all his wits about him, emphatically showed his disapproval of the turn that things were taking. Justly and shrewdly did he recognize the fact that the Church was appropriating to herself more than was her due, was definitely substituting herself and her interests for those of the secret of Jesus.

CHAPTER X

THE ARIAN HERESY AND THE ATHANASIAN CREED

It was the appearance of the Arian heresy which finally compelled the Church to put her beliefs in a definite form to which anybody might appeal. To survive at all she must provide herself with a dogmatic incrustation. This she succeeded in doing. The bishops, who were feasted by Constantine at the Council of Nicæa, devised the elements of a creed-formula that has been adhered to by the main body of Christians up to our own time. This formula was eventually handed down to us with more words but narrowed purpose in the articles of the Athanasian creed.

Arius himself was a man versed in smooth persuasions. It was ruefully said of him that on one occasion, in a moment, in no time at all, "he had drawn away seven hundred virgins from the church to his party." It is also reported that his peculiar doctrines owed their origin to the chagrin he felt at being excommunicated by Peter of Alexandria because of his association with the Meletian schism. If this actually was the case we have one more proof that nothing can sharpen the wits of man so much as personal spite. He certainly projected a fine harpoon into the church, a harpoon which caused its whale's body to blow, flounder, and spout foam for many a long year. His main intention was to establish " the unity and simplicity of the eternal God." Jesus in his opinion could not be said from the beginning to be co-existent with the Father. He was " perfect God, only begotten," but at the same time He had been formed out of " not being." Jesus was indeed superior to all creatures of the " middle earth," but inferior to the Almighty. When Arius heard it openly declared that " as God is eternal, so is His Son—when the Father, then the Son,—the Son is present in God without birth, ever begotten, and unbegotten—begotten," he not only shared with us the conviction that such a pronouncement was disordered, but he also held that it was blasphemous. However, in the œcumenical council convened at Nicæa it was decided that Jesus was " of the same substance " as the Father, and eventually, after several resuscitations, the heresy died out. Arius himself dropped dead while walking in the streets of Constantinople in the year A.D. 336.

The church during the fourth century was gathering strength and establishing itself. It was preparing for its long-drawn-out victories. Constantine recognized that politically it was a power. He looked upon it with the utmost favour and was not a little concerned by the internal dissensions that were disturbing its peace. The bishops were beginning to realize that the divine commission they were directing represented an engine of enormous force, yet at every start new theological hypotheses were being put forward. There was no conformity, no unity of opinion. The good men quarrelled. They excommunicated each other, they cursed each other roundly. Yet as Arius walked along the bright streets of Constantinople, and as St. Athanasius wrote his remarkable compositions in his desert retreat, the mystery of matter was existent to their eyes in her everyday temporal and eternal form. Each fragment of gutter-litter resting below the edge of the Byzantine paving-flags preserved intact its different actuality: the mountain glades of Palestine, of Africa, of Asia, and of Europe gave out, after the sun had set, the cool odours of the night, deep and rich and pure as the breath from the mouth of a thistle-eating donkey.

To envisage in its rightful perspective the gradual growth of Christian belief is a matter of huge perplexity. No ultimate mystery of life is known, none can be known, and yet ecclesiastical minds, under the pressure of hostile and inquisitive criticism, built up their involved and elaborate theology. As the centuries passed they were not content to offer their conclusions in the form of a hypothetical supposition, but instead assumed the prerogative of absolute judgement. Out of scattered and contradictory records, out of partisan predilections, and out of the hungry longing of the human heart, there eventually arose the thought pavilion of church dogma. Its outspread curtains sheltered men's cowering minds from the broad light of the unmystical sun. At the back of life, behind the varied show of the physical world, lies an unintelligible question, yet this in no way deterred these patriarchal priests from presenting with audacious assiduity their own pontifical explanation as the final statement of truth. They superimposed upon life their punctilious arguments, and by claiming a particular revelation entangled the minds of men in a purely clerical logic. I know not what to make of these creeds that have come down to us, creeds which, though originating in Jewish inspiration, have been couched in a style of Greek reasonableness. The seeds of their final form are of course to be looked for far earlier than the Council of Nicæa.

From the first the early Christians had placed their hope and trust in a belief in the risen Christ. The quaint symbols in the catacombs testify to this. Wherever those ecstatic underlings scratched a fish on the sunless stones of their subterranean passages they had in mind the words of Jesus, "I am the life." St. Paul himself says as much when he writes, "if thou shalt confess with thy mouth the Lord Jesus, and shalt believe in thine heart that God hath raised Him from the dead, thou shalt be saved." "I believe that Jesus Christ is the Son of God," was his own daring confession. From Rome, from Antioch, from many another city of Christian association the creed shaped itself. From a modern perspective the principal tenets sound strangely. Set against the long background of geological knowledge, against the thought-stopping infinity of astronomical knowledge, against the complexity of human psychology, this piece of bedside village gossip, not yet two thousand years old, has about it a singular childishness. Yet how many grave heads have contributed their store of knowledge to the wide arguments it provoked, what concentrated thought has been expended in justification of these fantastical fallacies. The inexhaustible majestic explanation that the church has raised on completely unreliable premises—how long will it last? There still to-day it stands, this imposing imposture, propped by the adroit brains of twenty centuries.

Hear the words of Saint Ignatius and imagine to yourself how they would have sounded to the ears of a cultured Pagan of an old Patrician house reclining under a pomegranate tree in his terraced and fountain-cooled garden: "Be ye deaf, therefore, when any man speaketh to you apart from Jesus Christ, Who was of the race of David, Who was the son of Mary, Who was truly born and ate and drank, was truly persecuted under Pontius Pilate, was truly crucified, and died in the sight of those in heaven and those in earth and those under the earth; Who, moreover, was truly raised from the dead, His Father having raised Him, Who in the like fashion will so raise us—in Jesus Christ, apart from Whom we have not true life." Slowly but surely was the error of Christianity implanted in the minds of the common people. And out of the faith of the primitive churches, and out of the faith of the early fathers, and out of the faith of the three hundred and eighteen bishops of the Council of Nicæa, and out of the faith of Saint Jerome, and out of the faith of Saint Augustine sprang the creeds that we are taught to say. The essence of Christianity is true. It truly expresses the wish and the will of human beings who in the face of suffering, spiritual and bodily, created this sensitive religion. Yet these rationalized statements are nothing, their provincial dogmatism is refuted by every hour. Religious faiths do not matter. Anybody, any church, can believe anything (as indeed they do) and it does not make a jot of difference. By reasoned argument it is possible to champion the claim made by any sect to the possession of a correct and exclusive creed. Catholicism in her worldly sagacity has understood well how to present and to uphold her answer to man's death cry. From the first she hastened to present her crude ideas in the subtlest forms that she could invent. "The facts" upon which her fortitude ultimately depends are often so disguised in unreal language as not to be recognized. She very early appreciated that there was a danger in simplicity, there was a danger to her authority. In a trice she had the *nous* to identify Jesus with the Greek Logos. Such metaphysical mystifications may be discounted. They are an unreal creation. They are clouds that float high and far while the real business that matters is being transacted on the firm ground below, upon the ground that smells of cow-pats, upon the ground where wood-lice perform pious errands, and where buttercups blandly open out their golden petals. Catholicism is like a snail. If you touch its tender parts it forthwith conceals them by spontaneously generating bubbles of air. It is given to using words that may mean everything or nothing. The creed of Saint Athanasius does not inspire a sane mind with a feeling of confidence. In it the church retreats so far into its maze of unintelligibility that it is safe from further attack.

Whosoever will be saved : before all things it is necessary that he hold the Catholic Faith. Which Faith except every-one do keep whole and undefiled : without doubt he shall perish everlastingly. And the Catholic Faith is this : That we worship one God in Trinity, and Trinity in Unity; neither confounding the Persons : nor dividing the Substance. For there is one Person of the Father : another of the Son : and another of the Holy Ghost. But the Godhead of the Father, of the Son, and of the Holy Ghost, is all one : the Glory equal, the Majesty co-eternal. Such as the Father is, such is the Son : and such is the Holy Ghost. The Father uncreate, the Son uncreate : and the Holy Ghost uncreate. The Father incomprehensible, the Son incomprehensible : and the Holy Ghost incomprehensible. The Father eternal, the Son eternal : and the Holy Ghost eternal. And yet they are not three eternals : but one eternal. As also there are not three incomprehensibles, nor three uncreated : but one uncreated, and one incomprehensible. So likewise the Father is Almighty, the Son Almighty : and the Holy Ghost Almighty. And yet they are not three Almighties : but one Almighty. So the Father is God, the Son is God : and the Holy Ghost is God. And yet they are not three Gods : but one God. So likewise the Father is Lord, the Son Lord : and the Holy Ghost Lord. And yet not three Lords : but one Lord. For like as we are compelled by the Christian verity : to acknowledge every Person by himself to be God and Lord; so are we forbidden by the Catholic religion : to say, there be three Gods, or three Lords. The Father is made of none : neither created, nor begotten. The Son is of the Father alone : not made, nor created, but begotten. The Holy Ghost is of the Father and of the Son : neither made, nor created, nor begotten, but proceeding. So there is one Father, not three Fathers; one Son, not three Sons : one Holy Ghost, not three Holy Ghosts. And in this Trinity none is afore, or after other : none is greater, or less than another : but the whole three Persons are co-eternal together : and co-equal. So that in all things, as is aforesaid : the Unity in Trinity, and the Trinity in Unity is to be worshipped. He therefore that will be saved : must thus think of the Trinity. Furthermore, it is necessary to everlasting salvation : that he also believe rightly the Incarnation of our Lord Jesus Christ . . . at whose coming all men shall rise again with their bodies : and shall give account for their own works. And they that have done good shall go into life everlasting : and they that have done evil into everlasting fire. This is the Catholic Faith : which except a man believe faithfully, he cannot be saved. Glory be to the Father, and to the Son : and to the Holy Ghost.

Who in the name of Epicurus could get any sound sense out of such a mare's nest ! Like a dead wasp, its most telling argument rests in its tail. It still reserves poison there. Any fool knows what " perish everlastingly " means, and " everlasting fire."

CHAPTER XI

ST. JEROME AND ST. AUGUSTINE

THE fabric of the church was at last built and it only remained for Saint Jerome and Saint Augustine to pave its forecourts and to picture its domes with golden tesseræ; the former with his Latin translation of the Holy Scriptures and the latter by putting forward innumerable treatises justifying the new faith in the language of philosophy. Only by deliberate action could the ancient Pagan civilization hope to save itself. Christian communities had grown up everywhere, as it were in a night. The secular world, except for a few short intervals of blind sleep-disturbed rage, had been drowsy. Scepticism had sapped its interest in anything but personal well-being. The indulgence that comes from appropriated wealth had rendered it morally feeble. It lived upon an ancient prestige, it lived upon its capital. Feeble in heart, feeble in hand, it existed with the semblance of stability only. There was a sickness in the body of the Roman Empire. That vital enthusiasm essential to the creation of winged life was no longer to be found in its service; it was in the hearts of the Christians now finally committed to the task of conquering the world. Little by little the religion was strengthening its hold. It had become a great cause. " We are men of yesterday; yet we have filled all your places.

It was making preparations for taking possession of men's emotions, of men's souls, of men's minds. "Who are these Cacodæmons," the great Emperor Trajan had cried, "hastening to transgress our commands?"

With the fourth century came recognition of the fact that the Christians had won the road to government. Yet once again for a short period the advance of their cause was to be deliberately checked. If Julian the Apostate had lived longer it is possible that the success of this "degrading worship of dead men's bones" might have been moderated. Saint Athanasius, that "despicable little mannikin," as Julian called him, was confident from the first that "this cloud" also would pass, and by the premature death of the Emperor his gift of knowing futurities was again seemingly vindicated. In the figure of Julian we are privileged to see the embodiment of the old classical world move sadly away. "That goat" with his bland bearded face may be taken to represent Roman order and Greek reason. He had been in close contact with Christianity in his childhood, and he had cause to hate this form of human oppression with a deep hatred. "The orator Libanius praises Porphyry and Julian for confuting the folly of a sect which styled a dead man of Palestine God." Of a philosophical and poetical trend, Julian turned back to the state religions of the great classical ages. He set himself with deliberate purpose to torment these fanatical spiritual maniacs who everywhere beset the kingdoms of the earth. To spite them he encouraged the Jews, whose "indistinct ravings" were so hateful to him, to rebuild the Temple at Jerusalem. He ordered the Christians to reconstruct the shrines they had destroyed. By his personal example in every possible way he encouraged his subjects to study once more the wisdom of antiquity. The old classical writers, "those spirits in prison," as Saint Augustine called them, were again established in honour. "The superstition of the Galilean" was derided as a gallimaufry of incredible legends, "a religion of threats and bribes unworthy of wise men." It is, in truth, satisfactory to know that before the inhabitants of the Western world were finally conducted by the priests into the tunnelled cavern of the dark ages, in more than one direction rational protests were heard. "The idea of an incarnation of God is absurd: why should the human race think itself so superior to bees, ants, and elephants as to be put in this unique relation to its maker? . . . Christians are like a council of frogs in a marsh or a synod of worms on a dung-hill croaking and squeaking, 'for our sakes was the world created.'"

The rude unvarnished truth is that the greatest, wisest, and most inspired of the fathers were responsible for much dangerous and foolish teaching even in their own kind. Their belief went to their heads as though it were sacramental wine too alcoholic, and we hear from their lips "no sigh for the folly of an irrevocable word." Saint Jerome is to be honoured as a lively writer and witty scholar. We especially associate his name with the monkish ideal of asceticism. Even in his own day, however, there were not lacking those who dared to call this learned man who lived in retreat at Bethlehem "too free with his tongue, uncharitable, sly, a hypocrite, the arch monk." In his work one constantly comes upon sentences that have in them an eager shrewdness. Who knew the

Scriptures better than this great translator who was diligent to hold consultation with the wisest Jews of his time? It was he who wrote, " All that we read in the Scriptures is light; even when we do not go beneath the surface. But it is in its marrow that its great treasures are hidden," words that could be confirmed, nay, that have been found to be true, by thousands and thousands of devout human beings whose highest bliss during their brief hours of consciousness has been to study and pore over this notable collection of simple and sublime Hebrew meditations. Yet by some he has always been mistrusted. Martin Luther wrote of him, " If he had only insisted upon the works of faith, and performed them! But he teaches nothing either about faith, or love, or hope, or the works of faith." There is a kind of unwisdom in much of what he wrote, an unwisdom which does not inspire trust. Listen to this grave utterance written with such authoritative sobriety—could anything be further removed from the sweet sanity of the earth? " I wholly disapprove of baths for virgins of full age. Such a one should blush at the idea of seeing herself undressed."

Saint Augustine, " that eagle of the fathers," may justly be regarded as the supreme philosopher of the early church. He was a born writer, and a born controversialist, and also a born mystic. Behind the artifice of his pages there beats the pulse of a living spirit. Nobody was more aware than he of the high beauty of the earth which he despised as transitory and insubstantial. It was to be regarded as significant only in relation to the Godhead " whereby the universe is governed, even to the fluttering leaves of trees." Void of such sublime innuendo the coursing hound would be nothing, the spider spinning her web nothing, the lizard catching flies nothing. Yet his æsthetic sensibility was always impeded by his sick soul. Saint Augustine's sense of sin stretched itself back into the very matrix of life. "But if I was shapen in iniquity, and in sin did my mother conceive me, where I pray thee, O my God, where Lord or when was I, thy servant, innocent?" Can the devout wonder that there are those in this "mart of walking sprites" to whom such extravagances of fancy are exceedingly antipathetic?

It was Saint Augustine who wrote the *City of God*, that great work that put forward in clear language the concept of Christianity as represented by the one single authoritative Catholic Church. This ambition had been expressed before his day in occasional sentences by the early fathers. It appears now here, now there. "Where the bishop is there is the church," Saint Ignatius had said, and again, "Wherever the bishop is there let the people be, as where Jesus is there is the Catholic Church." Saint Irenæus gives emphatic sanction to the claims of the domination of Rome, "For with this church it is necessary that every church should agree on account of its more potent principality, that is, the faithful everywhere, inasmuch as the apostolic tradition has been preserved in it by those who exist everywhere." Saint Cyprian boldly asserted that "Outside the church there is no salvation." Saint Chrysostom that "What priests do here below God ratifies above; the master confirms the sentences of his servants." Saint Jerome declares, "I, who have no other guide but Christ, unite myself in communion with the chair of Peter; I know that on that rock the church is built. Whoever shall eat the lamb outside that house is profane." Saint Ambrose announced openly that "The Emperor is not above, he is within the Church," and Augustine himself did not hesitate to write, "Whoever is separated from the Catholic Church however laudably he thinks he is living, yet for that crime alone, that he is severed from Christ's unity, he shall not have life, but the wrath of God abideth in him." What strange mystical shadows could pass across the flame spirit of this impassioned saint! It was he who addressing Christ wrote, "And sometimes Thou admittest me to an affection very unusual in my inmost soul, rising to a strange sweetness, which if it were perfected in me I know not what in it would not belong to the life to come." It is a pity that such experiences did not bestow a sweeter grace to his mind! There was an intolerance in him, a pernicious intolerance. Saint Augustine with his Catholic conceptions, with his elaborate explanations of Catholic doctrines, thought it no indiscretion to say, "The worst death of the soul is freedom to err," or again, "Better that a man's body should be destroyed than his soul." It would be hard to calculate the perilous import of so treacherous an utterance, an utterance the latent sentiment of which has been responsible for I know not how much human agony. Menacing indeed to human happiness was such a claim, and in the course of time when the corporate body of the church became all-powerful in Christendom it put into tyrannical practice what had been but a theologian's theory

CHAPTER XII

THE CONSOLIDATION OF THE CHURCH

SAINT JEROME died in the year A.D. 420, Saint Augustine ten years later. It was in their lifetime, therefore, that Rome was taken by the barbarians. The Goths had come streaming down into Italy to follow the standard of Alaric, and on August the twenty-fourth, A.D. 410, they broke through the Calarian Gate and Rome lay at their mercy. The great Teutonic leader did not live long after his tremendous triumph. He was buried by his followers under the river bed of the Busento, the stream being temporarily turned aside, and the Romans who accomplished the necessary labour being put to death, lest any of them should report the secret of their handiwork. Everywhere it was the same; strange, fierce, ignorant men from far northern forests were pressing in upon the civilized confines of the Empire. Shortly before Augustine's death the wide province of Northern Africa was overrun by the Vandals under Genseric. An observer might well have predicted that a religion as sophisticated as Christianity had become would have been destroyed along with the Empire, might have foretold that so universal an inrush of churlish men would have swept this ambiguous and ambitious church from off the face of the earth. As a matter of fact the very reverse happened. Amid the confusions of the time this new incorporated religion became the inheritor of the Roman tradition. It is likely enough that Catholicism owes its long supremacy in Europe to the fact that with the fall of the civilized secular power it was able to offer to the uncouth, superstitious minds of the northern barbarians its own plausible exposition of life with all the prestige of the great fallen Empire behind it. Christian missionaries travelled far. They spoke with authority. It was they who had inherited all that was left of the learning and reasoning power of antiquity. Their creed was formed and coherent. Their rough pupils had nothing to do but to accept the faith of their betters wholesale. Where amongst them could be found a Celsus, a Porphyry, or a Julian, to argue, to criticize, and to confute? More than a thousand years had to pass before one of their number dared to swing them back into religious channels that were more in keeping with the sombre temper of their national mood. In the West, at any rate, slowly and surely the church took to itself many of the advantages that had once belonged to Rome. It kept its abstruse secrets close. "For the multitude it is sufficient to know that the sinner will be punished." Saint Clement of Alexandria had written that "Christianity is the heir of all past time and the interpreter of the future"; his assertion was now proved to be true. Fortified by Jewish God-consciousness, fortified by Greek thought, by Latin organization, by Chaldean mystery, it was eminently fitted to adapt itself to its grand opportunity. It interpreted the future in the terms of the church. The future for the church was the church. The material natural universe was regarded as subordinate to the supernatural, the clue to which rested with the church, rested eventually in the pontifical hands of the " Pontiff of God, Vicar of the Apostles, Heir of the Fathers, Prince of the Church, Guardian of the only Dove without stain."

All vegetable and all animal life was of secondary importance. It passed away, man only continued. In the last resource he was dependent for his salvation, not upon nature, but upon a singular grace that he derived through the medium of the church. This grace was offered to the laity by means of the sacred sacraments which imparted its divine power, and also by means of the church's teaching, " which agrees with the highest truths of philosophy and science." The church offers instruction both practical and spiritual while it holds in possession profound mysteries which eye hath not seen nor ear heard. Earthly happiness is as nothing in comparison with the bliss of heaven. Theology is the highest possible science, and nothing should be taught which casts doubts upon its conclusions: neither should any action be taken by any secular state which interferes with the transcendent interest committed to the priests here in earth.

Such, broadly speaking, were the claims that were ultimately developed out of Paul's idea of a universal religion. In the East the Orthodox Greek Church separated itself more and more from the Roman ideal. It came to lay the greatest stress upon certain theological niceties and upon certain occult mystical practices of its own. The Patriarchates of Antioch, Alexandria, Jerusalem, and Constantinople were also jealous of their independence of Rome, and to this day these well-descended Christians refuse to acknowledge the papal supremacy.

When one considers Christianity as it was presented to the Middle Ages, spreading to the north, to the south, to the east, and to the west; when one contemplates its powers, its huge influence, its elaborate organization, its orders, its priests, its churches, monasteries, cathedrals, its vestments, its ritual, its liturgies, its immemorial customs, and then allows one's mind to return to the figure of Jesus walking through the ripe corn, or sitting amongst nets at the back of a damp fishing boat, one is dumbfounded at so strange a consummation. The human race, driven forward by its fears and hopes, willed this secret to be true, and its conscious wish having taken this form it never looked back. Steadily and surely out of the contributions of a myriad individual minds it built up for itself its great coloured dome of churchly thought. Generations followed, and what had been offered as hypothetical theological suppositions were, through custom and tradition, taken for granted as unquestioned truth. All the reasoning power of the Western world became concentrated upon reconciling the arbitrary conclusions of theology with the demands of logic. And under the reiterated assurances offered in simple language to the simple, and in infinitely abstruse language to the learned, independent and free reasoning was held as it were under a spell. Always from birth to death the people saw above them the great swaying mesmeric head of this cobra. There was no one to dispute the prevailing authority, there was no one who dared to dispute it. The rude German leaders listened to this theological ratiocination with open-eyed wonder. They accepted what they were told with the touching confidence of the uneducated. The little village communities ploughing their land with yoked hogs—how could they dare to dispute about such matters? The church was in the hands of men whose life-interest was devoted to its service. Men of outstanding ability, like Gregory, directed its affairs. The power of the church increased always, and as the centuries passed the actual visible manifestations of its presence over the length and breadth of Europe added what seemed incontestable evidence of its truth. For all over the broad acres of the West, among vineyards, beside meadowlands, and in mountain valleys, churches and cathedrals rose up from the ground. That a child should have its forehead marked with the sign of the cross, and that the arms of the dead should be adjusted to suggest the same symbol, became hardly remarked. Men were free to employ themselves with the importunate affairs of everyday life. To sow corn, to drink beer and wine, to hunt, to fight, to build castles, these were their natural occupations. The church held infallible answers to all inquisitive questions, and the church was the treasure-house of whatever culture had survived.

It was the laudable and declared purpose of the Roman Papacy to inaugurate a universal religious government. The kings and princes and feudal lords were to acknowledge themselves as ultimately subject to the Pope. It was an ambitious purpose. Rome proposed to bring all the nations into one single fold, to set theologically devised boundaries about all life, so that these barons on their chargers, these crossbowmen, these neat herdsmen, and pig-bladder tumblers, were to live out their days under the sun, as it were, by priestly sufferance. It was the priests who ultimately held power. It was the priests who could cast the souls of men into everlasting perdition. Centuries went by and the church settled itself down to enjoy its broad estates. It had become all-powerful. Few challenged it with success. The hold that it had upon men's minds is proven in a thousand ways. Consider the Crusades. Imagine the psychological state of the people who at a monk's wild words could leave family and home for so fabulous an enterprise! The church deliberately endeavoured to impose its priestly interpretations upon all life from alpha to omega. It was impossible, for the simple reason that these interpretations were not true. Try as it might to keep its fences up, human nature was always breaking through. New gaps were always appearing. The mental attitude of these priest-dominated ancestors of ours is amazing. They were like children in the hands of unscrupulous teachers. In reading these old chronicles it is impossible not to be shocked by the incongruity ever arising out of the juxtaposition of theory and practice. The Crusaders waded through blood to sob and pray at the sepulchre of Jesus, to whom their demonstration would have been as meaningless as it was monstrous. There was not even sufficient adult reasoning, sensible and humane, to prevent so tragical a farce as the children's crusade. Sacerdotalism was taking the place of religion. Wealth and luxury and worldly considerations were everywhere paramount. "They teach others to fast, and play the gluttons themselves; like watermen they row one way and look another."

CHAPTER XIII

THE CHURCH IN THE MIDDLE AGES

CERTAIN reformers, like Francis of Assisi, saw clearly the wide separation that existed between the gospel teaching and the practices of the church, and tried to remedy it. Occasionally, very occasionally, certain "red and bald" sceptics like Frederick II dared openly to challenge it. But the church had dug itself deep into the consciousness of village and city life. It was a dove with hawk's claws and could not easily be persuaded to unclutch.

The spectacle of existence upon earth—how amazing it is in its outlandish incongruity! Recall that beautiful scene in the gospel of St. John where Jesus tells the woman of Samaria that a time will come when God will be worshipped in no mountain, but "in spirit and in truth"; bring back to mind the simplicity of that scene, its utter naturalness, with the corn on the slopes leading up to Sychar, white unto harvest, and then go and stand in St. Peter's at Rome, in the nave of that majestic architectural argument, and watch the ancient Christian mystery being practised at each ornamented Pagan altar, and listen to the priests in lace with their deep stag voices belling to each other across the open spaces! Fixed in its rigidity the brazen statue of St. Peter, with its lip-worn metal toe, remains static still, alone the lovely

Pietà of Michelangelo contributes its human pathos to the scene. This statue of St. Peter is just such an idol as the old Jewish prophets were accustomed to rail at. It smells of brass. It cannot go unless it be carried. There is the Vatican with its doors guarded by soldiers dressed up in motley. There we have the centre of the hive. In and out they go, these men in black, while the only honest sound that comes to the ear is the squawk of a jackdaw as it settles on the high stone coping. Even in England, a country remote enough from the Holy See, there remain still on every hand material evidences of that deep delusion that had descended upon the lives of our progenitors. The rule of the church, the mental vision of the church, had come to be accepted as the natural routine of life. Its interference was taken as much for granted as, let us say, is the education of children in modern times. The Abbey farm at Montacute with its dovecote and grey gateway, the garth at Bindon, the arched ruins of Glastonbury, steadfastly represent the tangible shadows of a static past. Below all there has swept forward a natural uninfluenced progression. The Christmas lights at the high altar, the embroidered dalmatics, the genuflexions of the common people, the bells and books and candles, have been replaced. Farmyard dung impedes now the thoroughfare at Montacute where once the monks emerged to catch their carp; skeleton autumn leaves lie lightly suspended in the clear waters of Bindon moat; yellow mulleins flower and fade on the lawns of Glastonbury. When one contemplates the stability of Catholicism during those long centuries one marvels to think that its predominance was ever shaken. Its dogmas had the support of the keenest wits, its organization was unsurpassed, and there was no accident that was not illuminated or degraded by its sacred superstition. In hours of deep emotion men and women are driven to bow their heads. There are occasions when the most truculent heathen yearns to bend the knee, and in those years there was no dishonour in the practice. Life was established in myth and legend. Life was ordered from the cradle to the coffin by a plan celestial. Through the sale of indulgences, through the belief of purgatorial intervention, the present life and the future life were under the strict control of the priests. Young men and maidens, old men, whose bones cracked audibly like winter faggots, all bent down before wayside shrines of the Virgin half covered up with nettles. As each season passed a long series of ceremonies and processions accustomed the minds of these simple worshippers to reverence the tale of their redemption.

Last year on Good Friday, in an Italian village, it was my privilege to witness just such a Catholic demonstration. Down the narrow cobbled street the religious troop wound its way. Dressed all in white a band of children turned the corner, each one holding in its clenched hand some significant symbol of the crucifixion—a napkin stained in blood, some wooden dice, some rusty nails, a miniature ladder; and before a painted image of Mary, held so high that its head reached almost to the drooping eaves of the houses, was carried a bier with an image of a dead man upon it. With the chanting and the music in my ears I was held in reverent obedience. With uncommon emotions stirring through my being I tried to catch a glimpse of the white effigy. Well I knew it was no Apollo, no Pan who was lying prostrate there on the flaxen sheet. It was Jesus of Nazareth, the Saviour of the World! His head was turned from me and I never saw His face, only a portion of His beard. Yet that was enough. In that instant I came to realize as never before the overwhelming weight and pressure of this symbol of neurotic feeling. It is by the means of such appeals, of such melodramatic representations, that the free actions and free minds of long-suffering mortals have been held in check. There is great danger to the commonwealth of nations here. Emotion is encouraged to supplant cool reason, fanaticism to supplant tolerance. Not by such means can our race be saved. Here is no reliance upon heathen goodness, upon reasonableness and understanding.

It is the priests who have ever been guilty of perfidious quillets. At each chance they have contested the courageous conclusions of men's minds, satisfying their consciences by false contributions. Moved deeply as I was by this vain show, a secret and sure conviction came to me, emphatic and not to be denied, that the greatest honour was with that man who in the face of such overpowering mob psychology had rudely and boldly dared to cry out an unintimidated challenge. *Hoc est corpus*—hocus-pocus; dared to outface the Church of Rome, this imposing dragon dam of all of us, and like Daniel of old, to feed her with balls of pitch mingled with hair.

For there was a vulnerable place in the great structure of canonical polity. Presented as it had been with theoretically solvent arguments by many a subtle apologist, by Saint Augustine, by Saint Thomas Aquinas, and by a hundred other schoolmen, it even yet remained tender of any intellectual criticism. Well did these churchmen know that their large claims were open to objection, were, in truth, built up on insubstantial assumptions incapable of proof. It was this secret knowledge that was the direct cause of the merciless religious persecutions so dishonourable to the pages of European history. The whole fabric of their constituted power, both material and spiritual, rested upon an unquestioning belief on what had been taught. The mighty edifice was all-enclosing, each shrine was in its place, the swing of each censer was in accordance with tradition, but under the polished tiled pavements, under the deep foundations of this building, was a level of uncertain and shifting sand, *and they knew it.*

Little by little, first from one quarter and then from another, dissentient voices were heard. The Church was quick to realize that the whole constitution of regulated society which it had for so long come to consider as its permanent heritage was threatened. Its great vested interests were menaced, and wherever "the cancer of heresy" showed itself it struck out blindly, passionately, as men will ever do in the cause of self-interest. Its idea had been that the citizens and peasants should be content to be led like little Easter lambs from time to eternity, but "in time" there was to be no path of life where the authority of the churchmen was not actively present. Ecclesiastical interference was common in every department of civil government. These mediæval priests, these shaven pates, must have a finger in every pie. Vast indeed were the possessions of the church, vaster still its ambitions. There were men found to justify its most extravant claims. All roads led to Rome. These plump Abbots with bags of gold hanging from the ornamented saddles of their bean-fed pads—how could they ever be convinced that their world consecrated by the past was merely a chance creation? The impulse for material advantage had been so intermingled with purposes wholly spiritual that any lucid separation of the two had become well-nigh impossible. The Catholic Church was there palpably planted. There was salvation in it and there was also land in it. With so much at stake, nay, with their very vision of life at stake, small wonder that the cruellest passions flamed up at the first sign of contradiction.

It was the destruction of the Roman Empire that had made it possible for the church to replace the old classical method of free intellectual inquiry with its own hard-set theological theorizing. For centuries the Western world forswore men's highest heritage, their gift for unimpeded individual consciousness. Dogmas shut them in, and these dogmas had the support of the ruling powers both secular and episcopalian. Who could have predicted such an upshot? Yet the very success of the church spelled its ruin. Its strength gave it an unwise sense of security. It pressed its conclusions to its own advantage. Worldly considerations became paramount. That animate spiritual power out of which Christianity had at first risen was now estranged. Forthwith it set about to destroy what it itself had created. Now here, now there, rose up certain intrepid souls who steadfastly challenged the prevailing superstitions, and the passionate allegiance of these men had the support of a large portion of the laity who perhaps for purely economic motives resented the greed of the Roman Curia. This combination of spiritual and material interest, together with the new learning, gave birth to the Reformation. Long before the sixteenth century certain pertinent and subversive questions had been asked. We have seen how, even before the fourth century, the foundations of the church of the Middle Ages had been laid upon the claim of the Bishop of Rome to be the successor "of the two most glorious of the apostles." In the eleventh century Gregory VII had only reaffirmed and developed what was already an established theory. Thomas Aquinas had given to this same practical policy an intellectual justification. Early in the fourteenth century, however, we find Marsiglio Padua contesting the right of the Pope to control the election of the Emperor by boldly asserting that "the assumed supremacy of the Bishop of Rome was without basis, since it was very doubtful if Peter was ever in Rome, and in any case there was no evidence that he had transmitted any exceptional prerogative to succeeding bishops." This protest was made particularly apposite by the sojourn of the papal court at Avignon, and the event of the great schism. How could the existence of two popes be reconciled to the older teaching? Practical expedients proved prejudicial to the ancient conclusions of priestly polity. They supplied object lessons divorced from arguments.

CHAPTER XIV

JOHN WYCLIFFE, JOHN HUSS, AND MARTIN LUTHER

In thirteen hundred and sixty-six John Wycliffe was attacking the papacy on the score that it lacked scriptural sanction. This shrewd Yorkshireman recognized the fact that righteousness was one thing and worldly possessions another. In the accredited doctrine of transubstantiation he saw nothing but "a blasphemous folly." He sent out poor preachers to spread abroad the teachings of Jesus in sermons delivered in the common speech of the land. The hungry oppressed people listened to the words of these premature Wesleyans with eager enthusiasm, and behold! it was found that the teaching of Jesus had lost little of its pristine power. Wycliffe was not content; he translated Saint Jerome's Vulgate into English so that his countrymen could read the Scriptures in their own tongue. The patronage of John of Gaunt and certain political accidents of the time made it possible for Wycliffe to die a natural death. The church could only expend its fury on the dead bones of this good man, knaving them out of the grave forty years later "to beat the bones of the buried." The courtiers who came to England with Richard II's wife, Anne of Bohemia, carried Wycliffe's doctrines back with them to their far country. Here also they were greedily received.

John Huss took them as the foundations of his thinking. He wrote and uttered dangerous words. The Pope at Rome, he suggested, was little better than the antichrist; Wycliffe he judged to be a pious and an orthodox man, and he held that "in the things that pertain unto salvation God is to be obeyed rather than man." They gave him "a safe-conduct" to the Council at Constance and there they called upon him to recant; but this "pale thin man in mean attire" had the stomach of truth in him. Christ, not Peter, he asserted was the head of the church. The priests in the crowded room held up their hands in horror; solemnly they condemned him to be burnt, consigning his soul to the devil. In silent prayer John Huss committed it to the care of the gentle imaginary God of his allegiance. He was burnt at the stake. "In the truth of the gospel which hitherto I have written, talked, and preached, I now joyfully die." When the church had done its work the priests very carefully collected the charred ashes, pitiful in their silence, and threw them, together with the sod upon which they had fallen, into the Rhine.

In the year fifteen hundred and eleven Martin Luther, that monk with "deep eyes and wonderful fancies" visited Rome. To approach the eternal city for the first time is a moment of great significance in the life of any man. The sight of those huge fragmentary ruins would fill even dullard heads with speculations upon the past. These grey broken piles shock the mind with their tangible evidence of the objective truth of history. A vision is forced upon the apprehension, and a dead and ancient people rise again to re-enact their proud accomplished pageant. "I greet thee, thou Holy Rome!" exclaimed Luther as the city came into view. He lodged there for a whole month. It is curious to think of this arch-enemy of Rome going about her streets with the grave wonder of any ordinary traveller. The stones built into the girth of the Colosseum are the same to-day as when he looked upon them. The churches, the relics he examined, are the same. His mind, so eager for religious inspiration, was, however, profoundly disillusioned. The lusts of the flesh, the pomps of this world, were paramount. Mummery and meretricious miracles mocked the memory of pure worship. "But besides this a delicate and prosperous life is hugely contrary to the hopes of a blessed eternity." The church was given to chambering and wantonness. Nothing was held in so high esteem as wealth. "Put money in your purse!" He never forgot the impression he received during those days. "If there is a hell, Rome is built over it," he was accustomed to say. He returned to Germany.

It was the public sale of indulgences by John Tetzel that caused him to nail his ninety-five theses upon the door of the castle church of Wittenberg. He could do no otherwise. Master Tetzel, the mountebank papal commissioner, was a good salesman. "These letters have such power that they would absolve a man who had violated the mother of God. . . . The soul flies out of purgatory as soon as the money rattles in the box." In the time of the plague Luther's friends had protested against his staying at his post. The monk with grim humour had answered that he would not budge: "Not that I do not fear death (I am not the apostle Paul, but only the lecturer on the apostle Paul) but I hope the Lord will deliver me from my fear." The man was brave and no mistake about it. With the memory of the fate of John Huss in their minds his followers tried to dissuade him from attending the Diet at Worms. He answered impatiently that he would go "though there were as many devils there as tiles on the roofs." His reasoning was simple and direct: "If Huss had been burnt, the truth had not been burnt with him." Narrow though the man's sympathies were, cramped though his mind was, it is impossible not to honour him as he, in his turn, stood up before the churchmen and their Emperor, and said, "I am bound by the Scriptures which I have quoted; my conscience is thirled to the word of God. I may not and will not recant. . . . I can do nothing else; here I stand; so help me God! Amen." These "drunken Germans" were to be deceived no longer. The whole castle of Catholicism built by the labour of so many ages with lancet windows, embattlements, and dungeons was attacked upon every side. Great beggarly cannon-balls were sent flying against its buttresses, moles were constructed against its moats, mines were dug under its foundations, and its defenders were pestered with a thousand little fiery arrows. The efficacy of the Catholic means to salvation was now flatly denied. Not by any magical mechanic was this high boon to be won. The miracle of "Mistress the Mass" which for so many years had been accepted with content was now derided. It was little better than a pinchbeck trick imposed upon the ignorant by mischievous priests. "In the stead of the Lord's holy table they gave the people, with much solemn disguising, a thing which they called their Mass; but in deed and in truth it is a very masking and mockery of the true supper of the Lord, or rather I may call it a crafty juggling, whereby these false thieves and jugglers have bewitched the minds of the simple people."

It was necessary to go back, back to the first records of the religion, back to the gospels and the earliest teaching; and there at last, so these good men reasoned, absolute truth would be found. The church became "mad" with fury. "The great Lutheran fool" they declared, had brought together all previous heresies "in one stinking mass." But neither by wrath nor conciliation could the religious revolution be stopped. It mattered not whether the Pope addressed brother Martin as "dear Son" or as "bastard of the devil," in every village and town and county the new teaching spread apace. It was a deadly struggle, a struggle without mercy, but in the end the Pope could do nothing more. "Yet at the sight of the Old Man, that sat in the mouth of the cave, he (Christian) could not tell what to think, 'specially because he spake to him, though he could not go after him; saying, *You will never mend, till more of you be burnt.* But Christian held his peace, and set a good face on't, and so went by, and catched no hurt."

CHAPTER XV

THE PRISON OF PROTESTANTISM

To the reformers the situation appeared simple enough. The papal Catholic tradition had appropriated the true word to its own uses, had traduced the truth to its own ends. In a public garden at Geneva there may be seen stone statues of these dour religious radicals. There they stand inappropriately enough behind a pretty artificial pool with their grave grim faces: Luther, Calvin, Knox, Zwingli, Melanchthon, and the rest of them. I have seldom looked upon a more imposing group. Yet I would rather "go copsing" than put my life in their power or my soul either. Aha! what majestic moralists, what surly whoreson moralists, and yet it never struck their laborious, over-serious minds, no, not for a moment, that Christianity itself, in its primary origin might not accord with fact. Tenaciously, blindly, they held now to the Book. The writers of the Bible, John Calvin asserted, had been "sure and authentic amanuenses of the Holy Spirit."

To an outsider it seems extraordinary that the damaging reasoning faculties of these men went no further than they did. How is it that they saw so easily through the acclaimed miracles of their own day and yet never for a moment doubted the validity of such palpable fables as the story of the Virgin Birth and of the Ascension? And yet what a touching and profound testimony is here to the unsearchable power of Christ's immortal words! Though every image was shattered, though every altar was broken, yet His appeal of so strange and unrivalled a tenderness lived on. In their cottage homes oppressed labourers studied to get at the inner meanings of these ancient wayside utterances. They saw a new hope in them, a new salvation. Just as the teachings of Wycliffe had roused the peasantry of England to revolt against their taskmasters so now the simple words of justice to be found in the New Testament encouraged the lower classes of Germany to rebel. Small support did they get from Luther: "Have no pity on the poor folk; stab, smite, throttle, who can!" Nothing in the world is so difficult as to free the mind of prejudice and preconception. We live, each one of us, in the servitude of dark rulers, and our intelligence is ever at their beck and nod. Only indirectly did the Reformation free the conscious thought of Europe. At first its teachings did little else but substitute a severer tyranny.

The core of Protestantism may be found in the Institutes of John Calvin. This impressive old rogue—little, lean, and bearded—dug himself in at Geneva. It was in that lovely city of blue water that his disciples learnt from their master their glum theology. The home where he lived has been destroyed, the place of his burial has been forgotten, and when I searched for some relic of the man I found only his stiff-backed chair, his chair of judgment! He was another Moses. He liked nothing better than to forbid. He ground men's pretty conceits between his narrow grating teeth. All that was gracious in the Catholic idea he despised, and with the utmost deliberation he delivered the human race to a monstrous god of his own creation. Thousands, nay, millions of our kind, were, owing to this man's philosophy, beset by fresh misgivings. His God surpassed in frightfulness the most abominable nightmare of the African jungle. This being was the be-all and the end-all of life. He knew the fate of every individual soul from the beginning. All were deserving of punishment, all were obnoxious to him, the very babies slapped to life by the midwives were predestined for damnation. A chosen few only were to be saved "at the mere pleasure of God." The object and sole purpose of man's existence was to know, to come into close communion with, this hideous deity. If you had been selected to do so this could be achieved by means of the Scriptures. "There is an inseparable relation between faith and the Word, and these can no more be disconnected from each other than rays of light from the sun." Our confidence in the pages of the Bible must find support, not through the help of what Luther had called "that pretty harlot reason," but through the testimony of the spirit. Those only who "are inwardly taught by the Holy Spirit acquiesce implicitly in Scripture." Jesus came down from heaven to rescue men from their state of deserved damnation, a state bequeathed to them by Adam's failings. "Christ, in His death, was offered to the Father as a propitiatory victim." This propitiation, however, implied no diversity of opinion between the Persons of the Trinity. "Christ could not merit anything save by the good pleasure of God." His crucifixion was of value because God selected to give value to it, that was all.

Thus one crazy thought follows another in dreary sequence, so that those who love grace find that they have gained small advantage of this man's croakings. Yet by the very contradictions of theological opinions the theocratic tyranny of the Western culture was broken. Men were still burnt fast and free for the opinions they held. Yet the fires that were consuming Catholics and Protestants were also purifying the air. There was a blessed revival of scepticism, and with scepticism came tolerance. "There is no god, it is clear as the sun and as evident as the day that there is no god, and still more that there can be none."

CHAPTER XVI

CHRISTIAN CHARITY

CHRISTIANITY, there can be no doubt of it, has been but a dream that has taken possession of the human imagination for two thousand years. Many generations will have to pass before Christianity is freed from the cloying dogmas that cling to it, stifling the beautiful and incredible conceptions that have trembling life at their core. The compassion inherent in it will then be absorbed in the culture of the race so that the poetry at the centre of this childish neurosis will for ever continue to play a part in man's spiritual evolution. A certain tenderness, rare and disinterested, will owe its origin to Jesus. Something of it will remain for all time, mystical and persuasive like the smell of summer rain on a parched garden plot. The religion as we know it will surely drift out of our thoughts. Even now I am constantly aware of the romance of its passing. In a little time the cathedrals and churches will have taken upon themselves the proud, poetical glamour of abandoned temples. Men and women will enter them with reverent indulgence as they now in meditative mood visit the few remaining tumbled pantheons of the Pagan worship. The little grey village churches of England, with their square towers sheltered by rook-haunted trees, with their foundations bounded by buttercup pastures, will evoke in the minds of wayfarers poetical recollections of a devotion that will have vanished. Certain conservative and elect spirits will continue to gather at the altars of a dying cult. Generations will pass and they also will have gone, gathered under a benediction in the graveyard.

The other day I left the arbitrary brightness of the sun in order that I might, stepping through a darkened porch, examine the interior of one of these buildings. All was silent within. It seemed that I was alone, and then suddenly I realized that I was in the presence of a group of Christians kneeling in silent prayer after the celebration of their central rite. Here they were with their grey heads bowed in still communion. Gone in a moment from my mind was all my indurated prejudice. I, a natural heathen, had caught these simple strangers off their guard and could do nothing but retreat.

In a world where companies of instinct-impelled eels undertake protracted and arduous pilgrimages with justification, where swallows gather in restless excitement at the calling of the September winds, it may very well be that beyond all reason, beyond all discussion, this remnant surviving still in an age of steel may not without wisdom continue to put confidence in its ancient loyalty. A trembling in the bones may carry a more convincing testimony than the dry documented deductions of the brain.

It is usual, however, to bring forward an emotion common to mankind as evidence of the truth of any particular creed. Lost in a universe magical, majestic, and mysterious, in a universe incomparable and incomprehensible, it is the lot of each one of us to quiver like aspens with religious devotion. The yellow Chinese is bewildered by this same trouble: the Indian under his mango tree, the black African in his shining forest scraping the surface of the earth with a sharpened stick! These emotions accelerate our facile trust in the particular faith of our environment. At the first attempt we make to put our feelings into words we err. The refutation of human dogma resides in the farthest star, in the spiral dance of stellar matter, in the material unconcern of moon crevices, in the open eyes of a fish moving through dark waters at the bottom of the Atlantic, and in the emphatic amoral presence of a musk thistle sturdily thrusting itself up into the light of the sun.

I myself do not doubt that the good fortune of the human race depends more on science than on religion. In all directions the bigotry of the churches obstructs amelioration. "I will go back to my place, said Obstinate; I will be no companion of such misled fantastical fellows." As long as the majority of men rely upon supernatural interference, supernatural guidance, from a human point of view all is likely to be confusion. Left to herself Nature will continue to bring to pass her own inevitable movements. Over-population will be corrected by pestilence and bloody wars. National rivalries will breed international disorders. What we would deem necessary for the health of the flocks and herds under our care we deny to our own kind; thereby becoming the foolish accomplices of a haphazard and unintelligent life procession that is degraded by much avoidable misery. Trusting in God rather than in man it is in the nature of these blind worshippers to oppose every advance of human knowledge. It was they who condemned Galileo, who resisted Darwin, and who to-day deride the doctrines of Freud. Scepticism begets tolerance:

> Good and Evil are no more!
> Sinai's trumpets cease to roar!
> Cease, finger of God, to write!

Virtue is intelligence, is generosity, tempered by discipline. Below all ethical considerations and scientific study there lies a liberating understanding of wide charity such as was taught by Jesus. This "heathen" unmoral charity has been forgotten by Christians who lay stress upon their domesticated conventions. Virtue is the habitual exercise of reason detached from self-interest. The purpose of life is happiness, a happiness which can be fulfilled by a free appreciation of the natural poetry of existence. Accepted Christianity has habitually debarred men from this their rightful estate. It is not only the cruel hand of economic necessity that has disfigured the faces of the people in the streets. These insignificant countenances, so lined and anxious and contorted, are the results of sordid and unmeaning frustrations. With the acceptance of Christianity as an organized creed-ridden religion something unnatural entered into the world. The secret of Jesus has done a little good, but its false presentation a great deal of evil. By a fortunate dispensation we shall now soon be rid of these accretions. The claim of the churches to have knowledge outside of human experience has been a mischievous abuse. Nobody is in a position to assert that there is any individual life after death. There exists no proof of this. When closely examined the evidence for it appears infantile. The dead never come back to us, their "glorified bodies" moulder in silence and are soon reassured by the presence of our own bones and the bones of our children and of our children's children. We look down upon our dead and mutter the words of our religion. We affirm our "sure and certain hope" in immortality, as we have been taught to do, and then before it can be vindicated, before a score of curlew generations have whistled in the night sky above our heads, the confident priest and the confident congregation are themselves in the same case, dead men out of mind. The bishop in his lawn sleeves knows no more of this matter than the hob-nailed shepherd staking hurdles in muddy ground.

CHAPTER XVII

CHRISTIAN CONCEPTIONS

"SINCE therefore the most sublime efforts of philosophy can extend no further than feebly to point out the desire, the hope, or, at most, the probability of a future state, there is nothing, except a divine revelation, that can ascertain the existence and describe the condition of the invisible country which is destined to receive the souls of men after the separation from the body." But see how these necromancers have worked on our fears from the beginning, see how they have exploited the human aptitude for cosmic frights. That sturdy writer, Mr. Edmund Haynes, in his book, *The Belief of Personal Immortality*, gives us an interesting collection of churchly and clerical pronouncements upon the existence of hell. I venture to transcribe a few of them: "At that, the greatest of all spectacles, how shall I admire, how laugh, how rejoice, how exult, when I behold so many proud monarchs groaning in the abyss of darkness? So many magistrates liquefying in fiercer flames than they ever kindled against the cross; so many sage philosophers blushing in red-hot fires with their deluded pupils; so many musicians more tuneful than ever in the expression of their woe; so many dancers tripping more nimble from anguish than ever before from applause." —Tertullian.

"That the saints may enjoy their beatitude more fully, a perfect sight is granted to them of the punishment of the damned."—Saint Thomas Aquinas.

Even in our own day the Reverend Father Furness writes: "Look at that girl, what a terrible dress she has on; it is made of fire. She wears a bonnet of fire, which is pressed down all over her head. It scorches the skull and melts the brain. See, she is on fire from head to foot. If she were here, she would be burnt to death in a moment; but she is in hell where fire burns, but does not kill. Look at that boy. Listen. There is a sound like a boiling kettle. What does it mean? It means this; the blood is boiling in the boy's veins. The brains are boiling in his head. The marrow is boiling in his bones. . . . Hear how that baby screams, see how it twists itself about. It beats its head against the roof of the oven. It stamps its little feet upon the floor. On its face is an expression of the most appalling despair."

CHAPTER XVIII

THE PASSING OF CHRISTIANITY

CHRISTIANITY has held the field "for a time, times and a half." This moribund religion interferes with a clear and enlightened vision of life. We have pretended long enough. Christianity is but a dream of savagery and pitifulness. Beyond the clouds that are blown about the earth's surface there is none that wots of it. It has no validity in the outer spaces. The wide, drifting stars of the galactic stream know naught of it.

I have stood under a minaret in Turkey and heard the *azan* called in the empty blaze of noon. In the elephant forests of Africa I have seen negroes occupied after the same manner. Narrowly, on more than one occasion, I have watched our Western priests holding up the Host. The Indian, the men of China, none of them has known better than to raise sinew-lean arms to the heavens. It does not avail. It never has availed. Let the mind of man vaunt itself as it may, cosmic matter presents always her grand impeachment. We take too much upon ourselves. If purpose there be it is in no way concerned with us.

The human race has suffered three grave humiliations: when Copernicus showed that the earth was not the centre of the universe; when Darwin proved that man's origin was not the result of a direct creation; when Freud explained that man was not the master of his own thoughts and actions. It must endure an increment of ignominy before it will be prepared to temper its demands. "Nothing is in the intellect that was not before in the senses." In the monstrous matrix of matter how fallible and paltry appears the miracle of mentality. "For not only would all reason come to naught, even life itself would be immediately overthrown unless you dare to trust the senses."

We examine and tabulate and deduce our conclusions. We use the brain to our own bewilderment. Our throats swell with pride as we blow out our bladder cheeks. We have small reason for any complacence. Deceptive instruments though our senses be, we can at least with them measure, and weigh, and check up our practical summaries. We need not trouble our heads any longer about heaven and hell. It would be to our detriment to rely too much upon our transcendental perfidies. Better forswear such hallucinations of consciousness. We are surrounded by mystery, that is all we know and all we shall ever know.

We need not look for luck. The black rag I saw to-day, soiled and trodden upon, in Powell's Walk, behind Chiswick Church, is as much part of matter as is Hogarth's mouldering skull, or indeed, as is the farthest star of our universe, "finite and unbounded." The very body of Jesus was only known by inference. A myriad atoms, a myriad protons and electrons, diminutive and immaculate, danced within its animate beauty. Gods and men, we are symbols and shadows all. A swan preening her argent feathers on a bank of riverside slime for all her seeming composure is herself outside actuality. Relativity is everywhere. Time can contract, space bend. We live like dreamers startled to wakefulness by a sudden light. Only in glimpsing moments can we be persuaded to entertain any objective reflections upon our hap. We make our calculations from our own doorsteps and nasturtium paths. We cannot be expected to do otherwise. It is sufficient only to think and vast cumuli of disaster float uncertainly into our vision.

In hours of deep emotion, in hours when danger threatens those we love, we chatter out uneasily the names of invented gods. We were wiser and we held our tongues. There is none to save, there is none who cares to save us. Time and chance happeneth to all men. From cradle to coffin is but a moment, though our span be eighty in number. Though we catch our tears never so diligently in bottles there is none to mark them. Darkness obliterates all. Our natural proneness to forget has its culmination in the oblivion of the grave. A few generations of human beings may be buried with their arms crooked upon their breasts, but the practice with its tender associations has had no significance outside our village boundaries. Generations will pass, centuries will pass, and Christianity will dissolve back into mist. Even though we are frightened, even though we are broken, even though our heads are bowed, it is prudent to disregard it. Christianity is impotent. Deliverance cannot come of it. A wise man can do no better than to turn from the churches and look up through the airy majesty of the wayside trees with exultation, with resignation, at the unconquerable unimplicated sun.